THE MOM ECONOMY

THE
MOM
ECONOMY

The Mothers' Guide to Getting Family-Friendly Work

Elizabeth Wilcox

Foreword by Elizabeth Berger, M.D.

BERKLEY BOOKS, NEW YORK

B

A Berkley Book
Published by The Berkley Publishing Group
A division of Penguin Group (USA) Inc.
375 Hudson Street
New York, New York 10014

This book is an original publication of The Berkley Publishing Group.

While the author has made every effort to provide accurate telephone numbers and
Internet addresses at the time of publication, neither the publisher nor the author
assumes any responsibility for errors, or for changes that occur after publication.

Copyright © 2003 by Elizabeth Wilcox.
Cover design by George Long.
Text design by Kristin del Rosario.

PRINTING HISTORY
Berkley trade paperback edition / September 2003

Library of Congress Cataloging-in-Publication Data

Wilcox, Elizabeth, 1967–
The mom economy: the mothers' guide to getting
family-friendly work / Elizabeth Wilcox.
p.   cm.
Includes bibliographical references.
ISBN 0-425-19184-2 (pbk.)
1. Vocational guidance for women.   2. Work and family.   3. Working mothers.
4. Self-employed women.   5. Job hunting.   I. Title.

HF5382.6.W55   2003
650.14'085'2—dc21   2003052218

PRINTED IN THE UNITED STATES OF AMERICA

10   9   8   7   6   5   4   3   2   1

To
Zoe, Ben, and Oliver

ACKNOWLEDGMENTS

I'd like to thank the hundreds of knowledgeable mothers who shared insights and experience and who are the foundation of this book. Your belief in this book's mission and your willingness to support it were instrumental. Your wisdom fills these pages and is evident in the voices of Claudia, Agatha, Althea, Kristi, Georgina, Cloe, Carolyn, Cassandra, Sarah, Samantha, Eleanor, Missy, Kelsey, Caroline, Tanya, Beatrice, Kathy, Isadora, Lonnie, Julia, Kate, Helen, Hillary, Hayley, Charlotte, Jane, Jessica, Marina, Leona, Barbara, Annabelle, Megan, Eve, Marianne, Mary, Monica, Liz, Molly, McKenzie, Jade, Lea, Virginia, Rachel, Shannon, Cheryl, Stephanie, Ellen, Maggie, Teresa, Emily, Valerie, Veronica, Kylie, Claire, and all the others. Thanks too in this regard to Rita Allen of Gatti and Associates; Amilya Antonetti; Katherine Sansone; Donna Dees Thomases; my mother, Barbara Wilcox; and my sisters and sisters-in-law—all inspirations.

Special thanks to all those who provided and facilitated knowledge vital to this work. Among those many people are Gabrielle Barry, Kristen Bowl, Anne Boyle, Mai Browne, Jeff Coombs, Nicky Coolberth, Karen Demartine, Naomi Drew, Richard Diedrich, Natalie Gahrmann, Nancy Gruver, Elizabeth W. Hallinan, Jay Kansky, Joe Kelley, Richard Knowdell, Kathleen Kreis, Amy Logan, Lisa Miller, Seth Moeller, Karen Noble, Pat O'Brien, Monica Roper, Kathleen Shelby, Bruce Tulgan, Jim Sinocchi, Jim Waller, and Anne Ziff.

My gratitude also extends to those people who helped get *The Mom Economy* off the ground. Particular thanks to Ken Brooks, Bob Diforio, Maura Phelan, and Jerry Stevens at Childcare Systems of America. Special thanks to Wendy Packer for her continued support, unabated enthusiasm, and well-considered advice. Thank you Coleen O'Shea, my agent, for your astute direction, for believing in this book, and for so successfully convincing others to do the same. Thanks to career coach and work/life specialist Virginia Byrd of Career Balance in Encinitas, California, for your enthusiasm, support, and resourcefulness. Thank you Elizabeth Berger for being the supportive, candid, intelligent, literary, demanding, open, and unwavering person that you were to me in the course of writing this book. Thank you Denise Silvestro for persevering in difficult times, being my advocate, and striving to meet deadlines without sacrificing the work's integrity. Thank you Martha Bushko for your unwavering support in those efforts. Thanks to dear friend Dorothea Herrey for never doubting once that this book would come to be and for doing everything in your power to get it there. Thank you Lucian for supporting what I do and loving who I am.

CONTENTS

Contents

11. Telecommuting — 134

12. Part-Time Work — 148

13. Being Your Own Boss — 164

STEP FOUR Get Family-Friendly Work

14. Plan Your Search — 185

15. Assess the Job — 206

16. Negotiate Family-Friendly Work — 221

17. Maintain Your Family-Friendly Career — 239

FOREWORD

As a child psychiatrist, I see many families struggling with the stresses of working moms—women pulled in too many directions by the competing demands of the workplace and their wish to be authentically present for their children. But, fortunately, help is at hand for a large number of women needing to establish a better balance between their families and their jobs. The key is family-friendly work, and Elizabeth Wilcox has written an immensely helpful, practical guide to finding it.

The Mom Economy is really two books in one. In a lively, accessible style, Wilcox communicates a treasure-trove of sophisticated insights into crucial specifics of job finding, such as benefit packages, negotiating strategies, and networking approaches. Clearly, this is a savvy mentor who understands how businesses succeed and how people succeed in business. The breadth of these discussions and the cagey realism that Wilcox brings to them are alone worth the price of the book.

What makes *The Mom Economy* unique is that apart from convey-
ing valuable information, it also functions as a workbook, moving the
reader (pencil in hand) through stages of defining and refining her
own system of values, skills, priorities, and goals. Wilcox never loses
sight of the core dedication in every mother's heart—to give her children the very best start in life, in every way that she can. All concrete
decisions of lifestyle and workplace are in this sense not ends in themselves but means to an end—enhancing the quality of the relationship between mother and child. At the same time, however, the
author makes it clear that *how* this end is achieved will be a unique
and hard-won solution, different for every family and every mother.

The Mom Economy leads the reader through four domains, formu-
lating an inventory of needs, strengths, options, and specific plans.
This path brings refreshing clarity and focus to a woman's search—
what might otherwise remain a confusing muddle of personal dissat-
isfactions or impossible aspirations. Through the process, Wilcox
encourages the reader to make realistic assessments and decisions
through mastery of relevant facts and through acceptance of the bed-
rock truth that, lacking a magic wand, some compromises are likely to
be necessary in the workplace as in any adult enterprise.

This is a book well planted in reality—the realities of any mother's
commitment to do right by her children as well as the realities of divorce, unexpected disability, and the vagaries of economic upswings
and downturns. Wilcox's sources include interviews with a variety of
experts; surveys of hundreds of women; and considerable life experiences as a journalist, wife, and mother. Refreshingly absent are
polemical ideological manifestos claiming that a woman must utterly devote herself to her home or utterly devote herself to crashing
through the glass ceiling into top management. Instead, there is
cheerful encouragement, recognition of the enormous diversity of
situations presented by real women's lives, and insistence on flexibility and honesty. This book inspires the best in the working
mother, but not by floating airy platitudes, promising that somehow

anyone should be able to do everything. This book charts a path to fulfillment amid real-life uncertainties, and helps you use your wits to "deliver the goods" at the workplace, for yourself, and for those you love.

Elizabeth Berger, M.D.,
author of *Raising Children with Character*

INTRODUCTION

It was a winter's noon, snow like a white duvet encased her daughter's school. Claire pulled into the preschool lot early, unfurling a morning newspaper from a mud-drenched bag. Four months ago, Claire had quit her job so she could spend more time with her two daughters, ages four and six. To help pay her bills, Claire had recently secured two freelance projects that drew on her sales and marketing experience with women's magazines. Now, she worked mornings, evenings, and whenever else her self-employed husband could oversee the kids. As she had in the past, Claire would soon change her job situation, increasing her time commitment at work so she could meet more pressing financial and professional needs. In fact, a year later she turned one of her client's projects into full-time, flexible-hour work. A year after that, her work changed again. But for now, she was an at-home worker and mom, squeezing precious minutes from an early arrival at school.

As she got out of her car, I spoke to her about this book. It wasn't a new topic for her. Several months before, I had mentioned the book in passing as we had unbundled our children at school. "I've spent my life in magazines," Claire commented in response. "I know a lot of people. Bear me in mind if you want help." Throughout the following months, Claire would occasionally touch base with me, asking how the book was progressing, leaving a message on my answering machine if a relevant newspaper article caught her eye. She became a pivotal force in the early stages of the book, inspiring me to press ahead, alerting me to conferences on issues affecting working women, passing me a contact that she thought could help. She seemed to believe in her heart, even before I outlined my book to her, that the mom in the big blue van with the three small kids was just as likely to have a good idea as the man in the black suit. If women are estimated to control about 80% of household spending,[1] why wouldn't they know what kind of Volvo would sell or how to recognize a good book idea?

The Women in This Book

Claire is one of many women whose insights and support form the foundation of this book. She, like many others, is a valuable contributor, both in terms of the insights she provides and the experiences she recounts. Of course, each of the women's stories is, in some ways, unique. Claire, for example, has held approximately 12 jobs in 20 years, each move precipitated by one of a long list of personal reasons—a sick father, a newborn, a husband launching a home-based business, financial concerns, and a child entering elementary school. But all the stories are in some ways very similar, too. Those similarities are what this book is all about.

These women are not alone. The women in this book—and perhaps you as well—inhabit a sphere whose numbers grow daily. They are part of a large number of American women who are changing traditional perceptions of what a career path should look like, who give credence to one executive career coach's adage that "a woman's career is like a patchwork quilt, a man's a vertical line." They are part of the millions of women who now make up some 46% of the U.S. labor force.[2] They are part of the more than two thirds of moms with children under 18 years old who now work[3] but, like the more than 40% of married women with children under 1 year, many have taken some time out from the workforce to care for their kids.[4] Many of them are among the one third of women managers who will work part-time at some point in their career, primarily to care for kids.[5] Some are also among those women who account for 28% of privately held firms in the United States and are now starting businesses at more than twice the rate of men.[6] These women may work part time, full time, flexible hours, shared jobs, from home, or in their own businesses. They, like women as a whole, may change jobs more frequently than men.[7] But they have one common objective among them—to create a working life that supports children.

These women are, in short, members of The Mom Economy—a growing number of women with one foot in the workplace and one foot at home. And that's how they feel they should live. They cannot be defined by one term: *working* or *stay at home*—though we women strive so hard to put each other there. Some of these women have been stay-at-home moms and some have worked for pay their entire adult life. Some stand somewhere in between, moving in and out of the workforce as needs demand. And many cannot define their career under one single term. Ask Claire, for example, what she does for a living, and advertising, sales, marketing, research, magazines, publishing, all feature somewhere in her response. Because to get family-friendly work, women often have to think laterally in their search, refusing to pinhole themselves into one type of job for one single company for their entire career.

The women in this book achieve something that a good number of mothers want. Many of them change jobs without burning bridges, take less senior jobs but command good salaries, step out of the workforce and then receive offers to return. Ask how Claire does it, and her language is peppered with sound bites that a career coach might provide. "I am a specialist and a generalist. . . . My contacts are my friends. . . . I jump in and hit the ground running. . . . I come in and know what they're doing. . . . I'm willing to take jobs more junior to me. I say: 'Maybe I can move things forward.'" It is by understanding these women's strategies that you can begin to understand how to do the same.

How I Found Mothers with Family-Friendly Work

If you don't believe that family-friendly work exists, if—face it—you're skeptical of the whole premise of this book, you're not alone. To find mothers who called their job "very" or "extremely" family-friendly, I surveyed hundreds of women by teaming up with a Tennessee-based child-care organization called Child Care Systems of America, Inc., and by spreading the word among women's groups, women's Web sites, friends, friends of friends, and acquaintances. Among those women and among other mothers whom I interviewed and surveyed for this book—about 300 women in total—I found skeptics. When asked in my online survey what strategies she used in her efforts to effectively manage the demands of home and work, an executive assistant from Wyoming who didn't believe her job was family-friendly replied: "There aren't any." I had a similar response from another executive assistant from Billings, Montana. A marketing director from Portland, Oregon, concurred saying she thought it very unlikely that someone could successfully manage the demands of being a mother and wife with the demands of an executive career track. (There is such a thing as a polite slap.)

But among those women I also found believers, in fact many women who said unequivocally that they had family-friendly jobs.

To my surprise, more than half of the 200 plus women who answered my online survey ranked their job as "very" or "extremely" family-friendly, as opposed to "somewhat" or "not at all." Even more interesting, through their responses and through subsequent interviews, I found definite similarities in their approach to work. First and foremost, these women were on the whole unabashedly realistic about what they could expect from work and how much they could achieve based on the fact that they wanted a job that allowed them to spend time with their children. They were aware that what they had was greater than what they lacked. They understood their own needs and that of their employer. They were often good at networking, had well-defined skills, had a knowledge base, and were willing to sacrifice something—be it pay, prestige, responsibility, or even all three—to get the flexibility or reduced hours they sought. Most held a college degree.

The experiences of these women said a lot to me. From them and with the assistance of career counselors, psychologists, child psychiatrists, CEOs, supervisors, and human resource (HR) professionals, I was able to outline a process by which women could identify work arrangements that best met their family's needs, that were family-friendly to them.

Why I Wrote This Book

I came up with the idea for this book while I was on maternity leave with my third child. During that leave, my second child developed a blood disease in which he stopped producing enough platelets for his blood to adequately clot. His illness, combined with the demands of an infant and a four-year-old, left me feeling as if I did not want to return to my job until we, as a family, were in a better place. I knew I was happier when I was able to work in some capacity. I also knew that as far as my financial needs were concerned, I was lucky to have a spouse who could meet our financial needs for a time.

So I began to think about my skills and knowledge areas. As far as my skills were concerned, I had experience in personal finance and business journalism in print, radio, and even television as an associate producer for CNBC. I also had worked full-time, part-time, and from home and had founded and run my own magazine—a career magazine for college graduates whose content was carried by career Web sites like Monster.com. I was a mother to three young children as well as an editorial director of a Web site for mothers, and I have always had a passion for writing. Given that knowledge, those skills, and the network I had developed as a journalist and a mother, I decided to write this book.

The result of my efforts is a career book to help mothers get family-friendly work. It is, as I said, based on the insights of mothers and on the advice of experts in the fields of career and personal development. For simplicity's sake, it is divided into the following steps:

- **Step One—Ascertain Your Needs.** Step One helps you identify your financial, parenting, professional and personal needs so that you can find a work arrangement that accommodates them.

- **Step Two—Identify Your Strengths.** Step Two aims to give you leverage by helping you acquire an understanding of your skills, knowledge areas, and network. You may have acquired them through paid work, volunteering, motherhood, and/or at birth. Regardless, they are your strengths.

- **Step Three—Understand the Work Arrangements.** Step Three helps you understand which work arrangements will best meet your needs. It looks at the benefits and demands of full-time, part-time, and self-employed work and the options within those arrangements, such as working from home or keeping flexible hours.

• **Step Four—Get Family-Friendly Work.** Step Four is the culmination of the preceding three steps. It teaches you how to identify the type of job that meets your needs and takes advantage of your strengths. It then helps you assess the company culture, negotiate the terms, and maintain a career that best meets your needs.

Where This Book Will Leave You

When you finish this book, you will have no quick solutions. You will still struggle to succeed professionally while striving to raise your kids well. You will find that the person who doesn't need to work part-time often wins out (read on, it gets worse), that child-care assistance sometimes fall short, that prolonged time off can stall careers, that fewer hours can mean a diminished role, and that women with few skills and little education often get the short end of the stick (to put it politely). You will see that some industries, no matter how much they seem to have changed, are not amenable to moms. And you will realize that although the so-called maternal wall, which penalizes mothers, is beginning to stretch, it hasn't given way yet.

But when you finish this book, you should have answers. You should know how to prioritize your needs, identify companies that best match those needs, and negotiate for the job arrangement you want. Equally as important, you should know that you are surrounded by women—working at companies and working full-time while looking after their kids—who share your struggles, frustrations, and needs. You should be able to acknowledge, as Claire does, that reaching out pays off, that you can get the job that you need.

A Few Style Notes

• When I refer to third person, I use the feminine in this book. That does not mean that this book cannot apply to men.

• I do not personally assume in this book that your significant other is a spouse or partner, male or female. I have done my best to include all such relationships, but you may occasionally find inconsistencies.

• I have changed the names and other identifying characteristics of most interviewees for their protection.

• I acknowledge that fathers can play a very valuable role in a child's development and in a family's ability to juggle work and home demands. But many mothers have children who do not have fathers actively participating in their children's lives or participating in their own. For this reason, I have not discussed "shared care" of children between parents or, to any great length, ways in which a child's parents can support one another in creating family-friendly arrangements.

You should recognize that those in The Mom Economy—the growing number of women trying to put one foot in the workplace and one foot at home—can offer one another and the workplace a lot. You will see that The Mom Economy can work for you.

I invite you to contribute your thoughts and insights regarding working and parenting at www.momeconomy.com.

STEP ONE

Ascertain Your Needs

1

Come to Terms with Family-Friendly Work

Know what you need.
—ELLEN

ELLEN

Ellen is an affable woman, one of those women with whom you can pick up the phone and unhook time. She shoots the breeze like it's a twister, conversation turning with wit. She's forty-something, with two teenage boys and an attorney husband, and lives in the Midwest. And she's consistently held jobs that allow her to meet her children's needs.

"Flexibility has been key in the whole process. Whatever works," she says. *"Implicit to, that is, whatever works* now. *It won't be the same in 5 years or certainly 10."*

Ellen speaks from experience. She has worked part-time for an employer who arranged nearby child care so she could nurse. She's worked at home to care for her young kids, full-time on flexible scheduling, and at home again so she could help meet the demands of home-schooling her kids through the junior high years.

Ellen, mother to two teenagers from Madison, Wisconsin, on what a family-minded mother should consider first when trying to find or adjust a job to better meet her family's needs:

• Know what you need.

• Be flexible. Don't assume there's only one answer.

• Very seriously consider the arrangement you'll have to make for the kids.

• Make sure what you're doing is worth what you'll have to arrange. Sometimes it's very clear—we need the money. Other times, you may be better off if you take a part-time or evening job. Try to look at your decision objectively.

• Know the places where you're looking for work well enough so that when you ask for concessions, you'll understand what it's going to cost them.

("He was crashing and burning," she says of her eldest child in those years. "We could have a juvenile delinquent on our hands or we could seek something different. We told him we were considering home-schooling and it was like the clouds rolled away from the sun.") Now with her children back in school, she's looking for full-time work again.

KRISTI

Kristi never thought she'd be selling needlepoint for a living. Once director of merchandise for a major U.S. retail company in Illinois, Kristi left that career after her son developed a medical condition. Now, she owns a small, second-floor needlework shop that lies within walking distance of her home and whose doors she shuts at 2:30 P.M. each day.

For Kristi, the change has been significant. "I was totally en-

amored with my work," Kristi explains of the 15 years she worked at her former employer. "This is not generating the same kind of income. My intellectual challenges are not the same."

But running a small needlepoint shop is Kristi's definition of a family-friendly job, because it meets what she currently deems her most important family needs—the ability to be home after school for her younger son and to be there for another son who is now entering that mercurial stage called adolescence. While it doesn't provide her with the same financial or intellectual satisfaction that she once enjoyed professionally, her work arrangement does answer other needs: use of management skills, income, a local network, and a job that gives her the opportunity to interact. One day, she'll cash in on her network and the skills that she's gained along the way—but not yet. This articulate, confident woman, cut from a cloth that might seem better suited for the black and chrome offices of a fashionable high-rise, sits for now among needlepointed pillows, pictures, and belts because that role suits her current needs as Mom. Has Kristi made a trade-off? Of course. Is this job family-friendly to Kristi? You bet.

SAMANTHA

And then there's Samantha, a mother to three small children whose conversation moves unbridled through our one-hour lunch. She's worked at a large pharmaceutical company for many years, enduring bed rest for two pregnancies; coping with her husband's cancer, its remission and re-emergence, its remission again; and giving birth to twins. Over that time, she worked full-time on-site, three days on-site and two at home, and now "casual part-time" (no more than 19.5 hours a week) from home. She's clearly a valued employee, yet she has to work to ensure she maintains the position she holds. "I always overdeliver," she says. "I remind col-

leagues: Anything I get done is something off your plate. I try to not have them compare me to other workers. I make sure my competitive set is not a five-day-a-week office worker."

I stop her. Competitive set? *It's a phrase she learned at business school. Compare her against colleagues who work five days and her output will not hold up. Realize she's working under 20 hours with no benefits, "at a really decent price," and probably "twice as fast" (because of her experience and the lack of interruptions at her home office), and they've got a pretty good deal.*

And the conversation flows on.

So where does she see herself next? "It keeps me up at night at times wondering what I'm going to do when my kids are in school. But there are always new situations that you can't anticipate. It unfolds a little at a time."

Life Is What Happens When You're Planning for It

Samantha, Kristi, and Ellen are women I interviewed for this book. They are women all admirably tackling challenges like no Super-Bowl linebacker could—deftly and without the audience and pay to cheer them on. "Great decision there to go part-time! No benefits? Nice move! Good idea to leave the corporate world to start a needlepoint shop. All that salary, prestige—gone to sit among pillows in a small-town, second-floor shop. Right on! And Ellen, adapting your schedule to home-school your kids. Hurrah! Sock it to 'em, woman!"

Yeah, right.

These women, like the other women in this book, have managed to eke out jobs that meet what they most need as parents. They have what they call "very" or "extremely" family-friendly work. Line their jobs together, and they form checkered and unpredictable paths, paths tugged and shaped by the unsuspecting hands of the children they raise, paths on which the most ambitious (and even they at earlier points in their life) might frown. But onward they forge.

These women are what this book is about. This book is about mothers who realize that, yes, a raise can be good; seniority, nice; and intellectual satisfaction, rewarding. But they also realize that at times they have to adapt their professional lives to answer the needs of their family, needs that they can't always anticipate: a child's developmental needs, a poor school system, an ill husband, or even the arrival of twins. And at those times, the importance of pay, seniority, and/or levels of intellectual satisfaction may wane.

This book, if I've done my job as writer, will help you make the workplace what you need it to be for you and your family. But figuring out work that's right for you is not a matter of listing your career objectives and sending a shoe to your nearest employer with a note that reads, "Now that I've got my foot in the door, how about seeing the rest of me?" Finding work that's for you is first about figuring out needs. Then it's about finding that work, based on your skills and needs, and redefining it as your situation demands.

And that's probably why you are reading this book. You are reading it to get the same knowledge that many women in this book have—knowledge that helps them identify, secure, and manage work that's right for them; knowledge that can help you figure out *your* family-friendly work. If it's not, then go back to the store, return the book, and put that money toward a tray full of lattes (I can guarantee you, that this book will not add calories, fat, or—should you consume the whole thing in one sitting—make you unsafe behind the wheel).

Sometimes, these stories and the advice that they and this book contain may not be easy to digest. You'll see women accepting the fact that children can carry demands that bear a cost on their professional life. You will read about women like Annabelle, a mother of one from Rhode Island who is a part-time research analyst–consultant–writer. She says that family-friendly work is about "rebalancing your life and how you define success." Or women like Rose, a mother of three from Texas who works full-time as an assistant director for brand development for an investment management company: "I decided a long time ago that my career path would be different. I'd have a different measuring stick. I feel that being a mother is a major accomplishment. I look for work that allows me to do that."

But you'll read other stories as well. Stories like that of Stephanie, an executive recruiter in Massachusetts who has managed to find a job she loves within minutes of her home and who enjoys flexible scheduling and what she calls an extremely family-friendly job. And she feels that she has made no sacrifice in terms of pay or the level of success she has attained.

So Kristi Isn't Like You

You, like each women in this book, have a different set of needs, skills, and circumstances influencing the decisions you make. You might look at Kristi, that confident, silver-haired mother of two and ask how she could have traded in that high-rise office for a small second-floor shop. (Don't even mention Ellen's home-schooling her kids.)

If these women are not at all like you, that doesn't matter. What does matter is that you realize that these women have jobs that they call "very" or "extremely" family-friendly. They, like you, are mothers who want work that lets them be a part of their children's lives. When their needs change, they adapt. They share some of your struggles. That's why you need to pay heed to their thoughts. Yes, these women may differ in how they define *family-friendly,* but most share a similar understanding—conscious or not—as to what's required to identify, secure, and manage that work. These mothers "get" family-friendly work.

We All Need It

We all need clarity of mind. Or, as some suggest, transcendence. Transcendence is what will help give you the ability to step back and do what Ellen mentioned on p. 4. It will help you identify what you need. It will help you be flexible, consider the arrangement you'll have to make for the kids, make sure what you're doing is worth what you'll have to arrange, and properly assess the situation into which you're entering. It will help you rise above the petty and get a clearer picture of what you want out of your life, what you want said in your memorial—do you want to be remembered as an analyst of a successful company or the mother of a successful child? It will help you see that 12-hour day at the office for what it brings to you and what it takes away. It will help give you the strength to make the hard decisions that can come with committing yourself to seeking out family-friendly work, such as whether you need that level of pay, whether you can apply your skills in other ways, whether you can temporarily set aside long-held professional goals for which you've trained. It will help you define who you are, not let your work or your neighbors or your kids do that for you. It will help you see the forest for the trees, to have the wisdom to see what parenting and work and your life is all about. And you'll need to do that throughout this book. You'll need to have the strength and clarity of mind to decide what truly is important to you.

That need won't stop when you finish this book either. You'll need to carry that clarity of mind throughout your life as a mother. Why? In case you forgot, life is unpredictable and that unpredictability is played out nowhere better than on a woman's career.

You may not be employed at the moment, for example, but if you're reading this book, you probably are considering working again. After all, almost every mother works in a capacity other than rearing children at some point in her life. Similarly, just because you may have a full-time paid job at the moment doesn't mean you won't temporarily relinquish or downscale that job in the future. And even if you are currently committed to working full-out, that adolescent of yours who is suddenly acting out might prompt you to seek a work arrangement that allows you to be home after school. That toddler who is suddenly chronically ill might require that you take time off (like mind did, just after the birth of my third child). That job that you once thought wouldn't work might turn out to be the one you need when your partner is laid off. Chances are that something will happen. Note that many of the women quoted in this book changed jobs two years after I interviewed them!

What About Dads?

Of course, this book does not have to apply to women alone. "I think the unwritten book is how to get a dad-friendly job," a friend knowingly responded when I told him that I was writing a book on family-friendly work for moms. But it was his wife who gave up her demanding job as a corporate lawyer after she gave birth to their first son. They both had graduate degrees from Harvard University; but, for some reason, she thought it made better sense that she downshift her career.

Mothers are the basis of this book because it is still most often the woman in America who feels compelled to make work mesh with family demands. In fact, study after study has shown that working women, even those with working spouses, are still responsible for the majority of domestic-related tasks at the end of the day, from picking up the house to making sure the children are properly fed

(Did I have to tell you that?). One such study by sociologist Arlie Russell Hochschild (in case you're doubting me) found that, on average, working women with spouses still reported doing about 75% of household tasks. The women also reported doing more than 80% of domestic management. While husbands and wives reported doing almost equal amounts of educating and socializing their children, women took more physical care of the kids.[1] A study by Ellen Galinsky, author and president of the New York–based Families and Work Institute, found that mothers spend about an hour longer than fathers caring and tending to children's needs on workdays and two hours more each nonworking day.[2] Add to that sum the amount of time that moms take off work to care for a newborn, and mothers end up spending substantially more time caring for their children.

I found similar trends when I conducted my online survey for this book, for which the more than 200 respondents were mothers who lived across the United States. These women were from widely different economic brackets and had varying degrees of education, but about 75% of them said they were responsible for the majority of the daily child-care tasks. About 20% said they shared those tasks equally and some 5% said their partner was responsible for the majority of the daily child-care tasks. In other words, hands down, these mothers were spending more time caring for their children than were their partners.

The clear implication from statistics like these is that if mothers are spending more time caring for their children's needs, those needs will bear more of an impact on the moms' careers than on the dads'. That's probably why you know more women than men who seek family-friendly work. That's probably why you know more women who go part-time or take paid or unpaid leave after a child is born. That's probably why women with children earn significantly *less* than women without them and why fathers—perversely—tend to earn significantly *more* than men without children.[3] And it's probably a big reason behind why women change jobs more frequently than men. As mentioned in the Introduction, even the rate of women starting new businesses is now twice the rate of men. When asked why they went solo, 51% of women business owners polled by Catalyst, a nonprofit research group, said they sought greater flexibility, something their employers would not give.[4]

All this is not to say that men don't seek work that allows them to meet their children's needs to their satisfaction or that men aren't spending more time with their children than generations before. They are. Some dads are sharing child-related tasks equally; some are even bearing the brunt of these tasks. But even at a time when women make up almost half the workforce, women tend to expect their jobs to accommodate family demands more than men. That's why only one fifth of my survey respondents said they shared child-care tasks equally. That's the reason *The Dad Economy: The Fathers' Guide to Getting Family-Friendly Work* is still an unwritten book. As more mothers work and men take up a greater share of domestic responsibilities, such a book will one day be in greater demand. Not yet, but let's hope it will be soon.

Of course, it's not only women who are included in this book. In this first section, "Ascertain Your Needs," counselors, psychiatrists, and career experts—yes, men and women—weigh in with their thoughts, providing insights and exercises to assist you in identifying your needs. That input, as well as that of mothers, is the basis of this entire guide. So, hand the kids over to their father, grandfather, or unsuspecting aunt, so we can begin.

2

Strive to Support Your Parent-Child Relationship

*My children are happy, are doing extremely well in school and
feel comfortable, relaxed, and content in their life and on campus.
I wish I had more money, but I am trading that off for the whole
package and the overall welfare of my children.*

—ALTHEA

ALTHEA

*After graduating from Tufts in Boston, I married. We remained
in Boston and my then-husband began law school. I was interested in publishing or attending journalism school but realized it
would be wise to get the highest-paying job possible. I landed a job
at a bank in human resources. After a year, I was recruited for a
higher-paying job. After another year, I was recruited by an investment company. I stayed for three years and during that time
realized that, ultimately, this world was not for me.*

*At that time, I adopted my oldest daughter, had the conve-
nient excuse to quit work and reveled in being a mother for six
months until my daughter was diagnosed with severe brain dam-
age. That was the catalyst to propel us out of Boston and into
Connecticut. Depressed and lonely, and with our finances slim, I
decided to go back to work for money and therapy.*

We lived in the neighborhood of a university. Unbeknownst to me, my skills were desirable to the development office. I got a job in development at the university for four years before becoming pregnant with my twins, and, again, I quit when they were born. I realized that development and fund-raising was a very good field for women, offered a lot of variety, and that I had a talent for it. I also realized you could pick your field, as every nonprofit (environmental agencies, hospitals, all private schools, and all foundations, etc.) need development people.

I was thinking about going back to school for a graduate degree in historical architecture and/or history or writing when my husband left. Urgently needing a job, I went back to what I knew. First, I was director of development at a nonprofit. After a year, I moved to a small co-ed day/boarding school that was in my town. The job was a means to an end. Although I was working in a field I liked but didn't love, what the field offered my children was appealing.

After three years there I left to become director of parent programs at a small boarding school in Maine. As most mothers, I derive most of my satisfaction and purposefulness from my children's happiness and success, at this time. My turn will come later when they are well launched. I consider myself lucky, all things considered. At another time of my life, this lifestyle would have felt claustrophobic and small. As a single woman fully supporting myself and my children, it is a dream come true. We live in a beautiful home on campus for free, eat at the dining hall, and enjoy the fellowship of peers, their children, and the students. We are a community within a community. Because my living expenses are minimal, I can afford to maximize my retirement savings.

I still have to work very hard to be taken seriously and spend a small fortune in sitters for after-school care, work-related events, faculty meetings, and the like. Each year, the children get older and the whole picture gets easier, and I truly believe I have the best possible situation. My children are happy and are doing extremely well in school and feel comfortable, relaxed, and confident in their life on campus. I wish I made more money, but I am trading that off for the whole package and the overall welfare of my children.

What are your children's needs? It's a difficult question to quantify. Yes, children have basic physical needs such as health and nutrition, clothing and shelter, needs that elicit such questions as: Can you afford a roof over their head? Can you provide proper nutrition? Do you have access to medical care? These are finance-based needs that we will cover in Chapters 4 and 5. These are needs that an adequate income, a sound mind, and, if need be, employer-sponsored benefits—such as health insurance and child-care assistance—can help address. They also are needs that your work arrangement must meet. For if your job is not generating enough income to meet these, it is *not* family-friendly.

But there are other needs, too, such as a child's overall need for boundaries and discipline, love and role models, intellectual stimulation and play. Inevitably, the work arrangement you choose can bear an impact here. Think, for example, about a baby's need to feel secure and loved. One mother decides the best way to meet this need for herself, as a parent, and for her child is to take a year's sabbatical so she can hold and care for that baby at her home through the day. Another mother decides that she will be far happier and her baby better for it if she works 9:00 to 2:00 each day and puts her baby in a high-quality, on-site child-care facility that also provides a caring and a stimulating environment. Each may affect how a child develops. But you have to decide the best arrangement for you and your children. Yes, experts suggest parental care is best for infants. But many also suggest that if you're unhappy with the situation you've chosen, your sadness and anger can spill over into your interaction with your child, in which case you both may be better served if you work.

The point where experts do agree is on the importance of the parent-child relationship. That relationship is deeply intimate and personal. Children have a need for closeness, inspiration, sharing, leadership, and trust in you. And your ability to connect to your child and your child's ability to connect to you, experts say, is key. That, in the end, is the basis from which you can best judge and monitor whether a particular arrangement is working for you and your child. Don't base your decisions on how you're going to balance work and life on whether a study says it's best for mothers to work 30 hours at the office or 20 hours at home. You should base it on how those arrangements may affect *your* relationship with *your* child. Parenting is not a science experiment conducted within given variables. If you're working and your current work arrangement is in some way undermining or failing to support that relationship, it's time to reassess.

How exactly? Well, if you're coming home unable to connect to your child because you're too stressed out, then you've got to ask yourself how you can change that. You've got to endeavor to arrange your life to support your parent-child relationship within the confines of the financial constraints you face. If you're out of work and seeking a job, ask yourself what kind of arrangement will allow you to sustain the relationship you've worked so hard to establish—again given the financial constraints you face. When do you feel you want (want is reason enough) or need to be with your child? Are weekends, early mornings, and evenings sufficient? If not, where would you like to add to that? At what points in the day do you think that time would be most beneficial to you both?

Would your child benefit more from having your support when he is tired and having trouble coping or when his energy levels are high and you can have positive time together? If you feel your youngster is floundering, what schedule would allow you to be pres-

What Really Matters

If you were to base your work arrangement solely on what the growing number of studies suggest about the impact of parental and nonparental care on children, you'd be giving yourself a difficult task. Findings can vary greatly from one study to the next and interpretation of those findings can vary significantly as well. Because of that, you may well be better served if you take to heart one observation that studies and experts do consistently point out, irrespective of your child's age. Your relationship with your child is key.

Maternal sensitivity—how attuned a mother is to the child's emotions—is paramount, so is *child engagement*—how connected or involved a child appears to be when relating to his or her mother. Being home full-time with a child who has not yet entered preschool may mean that you can develop that bond more readily, but that's not always the case. Nor is it realistic to expect that arrangement is always viable. The fact is that many families can't afford to live on one income, and some moms aren't happy staying at home to parent full-time. Those mothers can still develop the sensitivity and engagement they and their children need. Once more, if the mother is unhappy staying home, that bond can be harder to achieve.

So if you are in a position in which you want or need to work, try looking at the whole "working-mother debate" in another context. Ask yourself what work arrangement will enable you to be best attuned to your child. Monitor yourself that way, rather than allow the latest study to push you into an abyss of guilt. Create a home environment in which you regularly listen to your child, respond to the child's cues, talk to your child, and show affection. If in that monitoring you find that your work situation prohibits you from being emotionally present with your child when you're home or to be home enough to develop that bond, then it may be time to reassess.

ent when she needs you most? Do you want to be home when she gets back from school? Do you want to be able to be involved in your child's school?

Questions to Consider When Assessing the Strength of Your Parent-Child Relationship

• Do you trust your child?

• Do you feel convinced that your child trusts you?

• Do you and your child actively admire each other?

• Is your child comfortable bringing up with you all kinds of crazy, dark secrets?

• Do you have complete faith in your child's good intentions?

When I started writing this book, a woman asked me what my book was about. When I told her, she said that she thought it should answer the questions I've listed above in more definitive ways. She wanted to hear *which* part-time schedule was best for children, Mondays, Wednesdays, and Fridays? Mornings rather than afternoons? Throughout my research, I grappled with that question only to find in the end that the answer could not come from a book. It had to come from a mother and her child. Women need to look at their mornings, days, and weeks and decide what would best sustain their relationship with their kids. There is no single answer.

You need to think about how and to what extent you'd like to be available for your child. What areas of their life do you feel you'd like and/or need to be involved in? Be specific. Do you want to be able to help with homework, go to games, volunteer at school, coach games, attend play dates, spend a few hours each day at home drawing or playing games, attend special needs classes? Don't belittle your desire simply to be with your child, whatever the reason. A few hours at home doing drawing or playing games may seem inconsequential in itself (perhaps far less important than the project at work) but aren't those hours on the floor watching your child learn, laugh, struggle what parenting is all about?

Don't Look Too Far into the Future

Also, remember as you go through this process that you need to deal in the present. You need to look at the child and the stage of the child's development and do what feels right *now*. Don't try to predict. Deal in the present and what challenges you and your child face. Don't trap yourself into a box of "what ifs." That's what mother after mother who has succeeded in finding family-friendly work suggests. Take Cassandra, a mother of two from Texas. In anticipation of her children's needs, she said good-bye to her financial planning career to start an interior decorating business two years before she even had children.

She thought it would provide the flexibility and steady income she would need when her first baby arrived. "Reality hit after I had my daughter," she says. She soon found her hours to be 24/7 and her income erratic. So she quit and got a job as a program director for a telecommunications company instead, a job she's maintained for six years and that is much more effective in enabling her to meet her children's needs.

Janice, a mother to a 10-year-old boy and a 12-year-old girl, has a similar message. She is a founding partner in a successful financial company. When her children were infants and toddlers, she believed they would do well in day care as long as the supervising adults gave the attention, stimulation, and support the kids needed and as long as she had quality time with them as well. But as her children moved toward adolescence, Janice felt that they needed the love and support, both emotionally and intellectually, from her specifically. She felt her personal presence when they returned home from school was paramount in maintaining a strong, nurturing parent-child rela-

Stages of Development

INFANTS AND TODDLERS

What are your objectives as a parent during these years? Do you want to nurse for the first year? How much maternity leave would you like? Do you feel that it's important to have the parent predominantly caring for the child during these years or do you feel you can share that care with a loving and trustworthy adult? Would you rather have that adult inside or outside the home? Are there occurrences for which you'd like to be present in your child's daily routine? Under what circumstances do you feel working can allow you to maintain a strong and caring relationship?

ELEMENTARY-AGE CHILDREN

What are your objectives as a parent during these years? Do you feel you need or want to be home before or after school? Do you feel you'd like to be involved in school activities? How important is that to you? How will you best handle child care over school vacation? How accessible do you want to be? Could you afford and would you feel comfortable paying someone to supervise your children as you worked from home? Under what circumstances do you feel working can allow you to maintain a strong and caring relationship?

ADOLESCENCE

What are your objectives as a parent during these years? Do you feel you need to be home before or after school? Could you enlist adult supervision for that time other than you? To what extent do you feel you'd like to be involved in school activities? How will you best handle child care over school vacations? Under what circumstances do you feel working can allow you to maintain a strong and caring relationship?

tionship. So she sought to arrange a work schedule that could support that—working fewer hours and increasingly from home. "It was easier when they were infants," she says. "Now that they're older, they need me more," she says. "I never would have predicted that."

The Larger Questions

As you consider how you'd like to arrange your days, don't forget the larger questions. What's important to you in your role as parent? What kind of parent do you want to be? Do you want to be a parent who was always there? Do you want to be a parent who put value in being able to support her family or who took obvious satisfaction from her work? Do you want to be a parent who was able to attend most of your child's games? When you are old and gray, how do you want your kids to remember you? Think about these questions.

Also, ask yourself what do you want for your children? What traits would you most like them to carry into adulthood? Are they developing those traits? If not, do you need to spend more time with them? How can you deepen your relationship with your children so that they are inspired to follow in your footsteps? Children, experts say, yearn to model themselves after the adults who are close to them and whom they admire.

Remember, too, that they follow your lead. If you return home stressed and impatient, unable to provide the empathetic attention they need, your children will respond in like ways. If you want them to be conscientious, patient, giving, and loving people and your work precludes you from acting that way, then your arrangement is *not* family-friendly, no matter how it appears. Be sure you are not so unhappy with your work and yourself that you can't engage with your children on a meaningful and mutually rewarding level.

Don't Forget Dad

If your children have a father who's present in their lives, encourage his involvement as well. A father plays a vital role in a child's development. Research shows that a father's involvement in a child's life directly affects a child's intellectual, social, and personal development. So, if viable, try to encourage the role of your child's father to move beyond "provider" as defined by a paycheck. He, like you, can provide much more, and you can help foster that.

How? Share the power, says Joe Kelly, founder and executive director of Dads and Daughters. You and your children will benefit as a result. "One of the few loci of power for women has been the home," he suggests. Mothers need to learn to share that power and to encourage fathers to take it on. They need to accept that the father is going to do some things differently from the mother. They also need to encourage the father to forget about strong, silent stereotypes and be open about what fathering means to him. "We have to stop this destructive cycle of silence. We have to start verbalizing about how much [children] mean to us, about how much being a father means to us. We have to tap into it. If we don't, we're squandering it."

Monitoring How Well Your Arrangement Is Working

Trust your instinct, don't predict, be flexible, and follow one other bit of advice that child experts give: Stay engaged. Try to stay abreast of where your children are. "Try to see life from their perspective," advises nursery-school teacher Agatha, a divorced mother of five children. "For toddlers, that means for me literally getting down on my hands and knees to see how they see life. For all ages, it means thinking about how they see life, making sure you don't in-

Is Your Child Having Problems?

It's difficult to get a complete list of questions, but experts suggest that if your child is demonstrating behavior that has you concerned, you need to get to the root of it, particularly if it's prolonged. Keep track of that behavior for two to three weeks. See what happens. Write down anecdotes that demonstrate that behavior. Be specific. Kids don't always verbalize why they're mad. If the atypical behavior becomes consistent, start to ask yourself and your child questions. Find out if there is stress in your child's life. Investigate whether everything is okay in his or her child-care situation. Discover what's happening in his or her peer group. Figure out what's occurring at school. Consult your pediatrician for help.

volve your own biases and personal justifications, it means trying to see the world in ways that are relevant to them, not you."

To stay better attuned to the needs of you and your kids, conflict resolution specialist Naomi Drew advises taking time each day to assess where you are. When her children were young, she would take a few minutes in the car each morning, radio off, to simply think. Don't resist asking yourself those hard questions. Do you feel satisfied with your family time? Are you unable to switch off from work mode into family mode? Is your work arrangement allowing you to provide your children with what you feel they need?

Don't Be Afraid of Change

Haley, who now works part-time as a partner in a consulting firm in Florida, was previously in a job in which she worked long hours. At one point, she recounts with audible emotion in her voice, she put in 80-hour weeks for two straight months of her toddler's life. Even when part-time, she found the work dissatisfying due to the diminished job responsibility and lack of career advancement potential (she had been taken off the partner track when she indicated that she wanted to cut back). She went through a lot of pain, she says, but ultimately, decided to make a change. To get a better handle on what she wanted out of life, she wrote a list of what she wanted out of her family/home life, decided on a community in which she wanted to live, moved, and quit. Within a few months, she had found another job she loved. Now, she says, "I don't get up in the morning without thinking how grateful I am that I am here. I took a leap." And, she says, she has "found something that feeds my soul."

You have to tell yourself that you can meet your children's most important developmental needs, but you also have to be willing to make the trade-offs that they may require. Just look within and be honest with yourself. What is your gut telling you? Reports one Minnesota-based mother of two who's a director of conferences earning $50,000 to $100,000 a year:

> Up until 18 months ago, I was a full-time vice president with a demanding travel schedule and an extremely high-pressure, and at times, stressful position. I reached a point where I felt my life was running me, instead of the other way around, and that I was losing valuable time with my children, who before long would be grown and gone. I credit my management with being extremely responsive to my needs. While I was obliged to give up the VP title and take a less influential position, I feel I've regained my balance and have the best of both worlds. My compensation is lower, but still very fair.

Sometimes, of course, the needs of you and your children will conflict. Among the women I interviewed, many said that at times they had to put their needs second to that of their children's. The sentiments of Althea—the mother who's quoted at the start of this chapter as saying that sometimes she meets her children's needs at the expense of her own—are not unique. Agrees one medical transcriptionist, a mother to two from Michigan, "I often wish I didn't have to work at all. But my part-time income does come in handy. I'm working at home on my own time, but I have very little down time. In a nutshell, I feel like this is the best arrangement for my kids, but not always the best for me."

Sometimes you, too, will feel that way. But that doesn't mean that the arrangement won't pay off. Take Kylie, mother to one from New Orleans. Her decision to go part-time was prompted by her six-month-old who was beginning to grow upset at the absences caused by Kylie's full-time schedule and her hour commute each way. Driven by her desire to be home with her child more, she had to negotiate the first part-time policy at her company. It was a struggle but ultimately worth it. "Since I've been home more my daughter's happy, smiling all the time. It's allowed us to have a schedule," she says. Likewise, Althea, who has three children, had no idea what life had in store for her. But now she's working at a boarding school, earning far less than she would be earning in her previous career, but meeting her children's needs.

Exercise

Now, if you're feeling so inclined, cut out the bookmark I've designed (on page 27), or make your own if you feel you need more space, and title it "My Family-Friendly Job." Think about each one of your children and his or her growth. Write down, based on the issues you've considered in this chapter, how you'd like to be involved in each child's life. Be specific. Would you like to be home when she gets off the bus? Would you like to have the flexibility to occasionally volunteer at school? Would you like one solid afternoon to spend with him? Think about what you can afford as well. Obviously, if you have to work full-time to bring in your full-earning capacity, something I'll discuss further in Chapter 4, it probably won't be realistic to write that you'd like to be able to be home every afternoon. Prioritize if you can. Now, if you've got time, move on to the next section of this book.

Real Mother Recap

You can create a work arrangement that meets your children's most important needs. Just stay abreast of what they need and strive, above all, to keep your mother-child bond strong. Give some thought as to how you can arrange your life to best sustain that bond, given the demands you face. Know that no scenario will be perfect, but when your child is happy and thriving and your bond is strong, you're doing all right.

If you need more help: Your pediatrician is the best place to start.

MY FAMILY-FRIENDLY JOB

My Needs

PARENTING NEEDS/WANTS:
(e.g., home for kids)

PROFESSIONAL NEEDS:
(e.g., recognition, certification)

PERSONAL NEEDS:
(e.g., time with spouse, running)

INCOME NEEDS:
(based on annual expenses)

BENEFIT NEEDS:
(e.g., health insurance)

My Strengths

TRANSFERABLE SKILLS:
(e.g., interview for information)

SELF-MANAGEMENT SKILLS:
(e.g., think independently)

WORK-CONTENT SKILLS:
(e.g., write press releases)

NETWORK:
(e.g., church)

Arrangement(s) I Want

☐ FLEXIBILITY

☐ FULL-TIME

☐ TELECOMMUTING

☐ PART-TIME

☐ JOB SHARING

☐ SELF-EMPLOYED

3

Determine What's Important Personally and Professionally

If Mom is happy, everyone is happy. Every woman needs something outside her kids.

—JESSICA

JESSICA

Jessica draws squares on a piece of paper as we talk. She's invited me into her kitchen, her work scattered about any available surface in her large, white house. The house is filled with her art— plastic flowers, curtain beads, shards of old Christmas balls, and other kitsch items that, shaped around everyday objects, somehow elicit a yearning nostalgia for an era I didn't live in.

Jessica's son returns home from school as we talk. He sits down beside me with a soft drink and a handful of Girl Scout cookies. His mother is discussing a big-name art show for which she had been picked to display her work. "It was hard on her," he interjects when she says it was canceled. "You're really famous, you know," he says. His mother gives an affectionate laugh.

Jessica worked 12 years in design in Philadelphia before she decided to give up that career for her kids. She had enjoyed flexible hours, good pay, and a boss who let her take extra time off; but over coffee at McDonald's one day, she decided her children would be better served if she were home. She had two children, Ian and Emma, three years apart. She had always been creative, studied architecture and fine and decorative arts. But during her children's toddler years, she found it hard to harness her creative energy to make art. "It's hard to be creative when your daughter or son is spitting up."

She moved out to the suburbs, and though she still was producing art, she wasn't happy. She missed the stimulation that a professional, urban life had provided. In the suburbs, though still an artist, she felt isolated and alone.

"It was a rough two years. I had this ego when I came out here. I'm going to be big, *I thought. And then I thought,* I'm just like everyone else. *She became depressed. She was plagued by feelings of self-doubt and sought medical help. After some period of treatment, she had an epiphany.*

"I decided I couldn't let myself fall any farther. I realized the most important thing in my life was my family." Through a lot of soul searching, she started to take pride in her kids. And she also learned to take pride in her art. "When I stopped asking myself if someone would buy it—when I stopped saying that—people started to like my work. I started trusting myself."

Now Jessica is successfully running a small business with 800 regular clients who want her one-of-a-kind works. She participates in auctions, benefits, and fund-raisers and has works scattered about in a number of small shops. She believes her position as a stay-at-home worker and mother gives her an insight and sensibility that large manufacturers lack and that allow her to connect with consumers in a way that others miss. "There's something wonderful about having a child's perspective, about creating a fantastic world," she says.

She's also happy with her life. She has been able to successfully channel her artistic talent, sales skills, knowledge of the design world, and network to grow her business to a point at which she can earn a satisfactory income from it. But income is not why she works. She has a husband whose job answers their financial needs. Her work answers an altogether different need. "If Mom is happy, everyone is happy. Every woman needs something outside her kids." For Jessica, that something is her art.

Where does your career fall in all this? As I mentioned earlier, the first truth that the women in this book bear out is that *family-friendly* often means lingering longer on the career ladder.

"It's very difficult to excel both at home and at work," says Richard Diedrich, an independent corporate and management psychologist. Sure, some women rise to the top and have children, but you can bet they have a tougher struggle making work and family life mesh than their childless peers. Take part-time: "Your career is probably gong to plateau for a while," says Diedrich of women who go that route. "You can make up for lost ground, but it's difficult."

So as far as your ambitions are concerned, begin by recognizing that if you want family-friendly work your professional expectations may have to give. Sure, some mothers such as Stephanie, who has a job as an executive recruiter that she deems "extremely" family-friendly, do not feel disadvantaged professionally for the flexible hours they work. But, as harsh as it sounds, it will do you a disservice if you begin your search for family-friendly work with that expectation in mind.

The reasons are twofold. First of all, despite what you might like to believe, face time is still valued by most of Corporate America. The person who puts in longer hours, who is willing to stay through dinner, sacrifice home life for work, is probably more likely to advance than the mother who makes it a point to leave at 5:00 each day. For many employers, the ideal employee is still the one who is wedded first to her work. Second, unless the benefit or perk you seek is the norm for your employer or even your industry, that benefit will probably cost. America, after all, is a market economy. Everything has its cost, including family-friendly perks that fall outside the norm. So, if you don't pay for these in reduced salary, you will pay in other ways—such as less responsibility, less accountability, less potential for advancement down the pike. Reconcile yourself to that fact. Many mothers with family-friendly work whom I interviewed did exactly that. Says Annabelle, that consultant from Rhode Island:

> *I went to an Ivy League college, law school at Princeton. Against how much I achieved in those environments, I feel like I'm achieving very little. But I feel like the needs in that environment have been re-placed by a happy marriage, watching children grow, participating in my community, in my church.*

But lest you think that women like Annabelle are by example advocating that women should sacrifice their career for the kids, that they should don their "No Place Like Home" apron and take their 1950s-style place by the hearth, think again. Annabelle is still making between $50,000 and $100,000 a year. She enjoys her professional life. She holds a high profile, participating in speaking engagements throughout the country, and acting as company spokesperson for the press. She maintains aspirations to increase the pace of her career when her children are school age. "I'd feel guilty if I worked part-time for the rest of my life," she says. But for now, what Annabelle has done is pare down her work to a level that satisfies some of her professional needs and still makes use of her skills.

Cassandra, program director for a utilities company in Delaware, puts it this way:

> *My objectives have definitely changed since having children. Before kids, I took on projects and job responsibilities at work in serious ef-forts to climb the corporate ladder, my vision of success. Now, if I can go to a challenging job that is part-time and flexible and affords me a nice living, I am happy. I am not building a career, I am not get-*

ting promoted. I am simply trying to get out of work what I need it to be for me. Period.

Getting What You Need out of Work

So ask yourself, what do you need work to be for you? Which needs do you feel work must address, and which ones can you satisfy outside work? As Jessica discovered when she started her own business making and selling artwork, work to her isn't just about power and recognition, about "being big" as she puts it (something that can be difficult to fulfill when you've got children wiping their noses on your sleeve). Work also is about self-expression, responsibility, accomplishment and security. At least those are needs that Kathleen Kreis, who has conducted numerous workshops on communication, employee motivation, and prevention of burnout, lists in her exercise "What's In It for Me?" To help you determine those needs, she has kindly agreed to let me reproduce an abbreviated version of that exercise here. Take a look at it. Once you rank your needs, record the top two or three beneath the bookmark heading "Professional Needs."

It may seem like a lot to bite off—evaluating your job when all you want to do is determine how you can get and keep family-friendly work—but exercises like these can help.

Why? Because when you begin to think about the type of work and/or work arrangement that's right for you, it can be helpful to have some tools to evaluate how satisfying that work will be. If, for example, power through work is most important to you, freelancing from home may not be an arrangement you should seek. If you want self-expression above all else, you may want to look into working for yourself or for an employer who values self-expression. (These values, by the way, also will be important for you to bear in mind later in the book, when you evaluate the culture of a prospective employer. So hang on to what you find.)

What's In It for Me?*

Not sure what needs your work meets for you? This exercise, by Kathleen Kreis, director of English and library services for Buffalo (New York) Public Schools, will help you determine what you want out of work.

"WHAT I WANT"—DISCUSSION SHEET

The six items listed below represent needs that work can fulfill. Rank these items *according to which needs you want your job to fulfill.* The need you want most to fulfill in your career should be ranked 1, the need you next most want to fulfill should be ranked 2, and so on until 6.

_____ Accomplishment

_____ Power

_____ Recognition

_____ Responsibility

_____ Security (this includes financial)

_____ Self-expression

Consider the item you ranked first. List examples of ways in which this need could be fulfilled in a job. Why do you feel this need is the most important to fulfill in a job? How is this need met in your present job? Or how do you think this need *could* be met in your present job? Think about your other rankings. What are examples of ways that your current job addresses these needs? Do you think another work arrangement would better meet those needs? If so, what would that arrangement be? Would that arrangement also meet what you've determined to be your financial and your children's needs?

If you have the time and the inclination, Richard Knowdell, a California-based professional trainer of career counselors—has developed a similarly positioned exercise that many career counselors find extremely helpful when dealing with their clients. He's agreed to let me reproduce it in part for you. His exercise, called the "Career Values Card Sort," contains 54 cards, the content of which are included on the following pages. By taking a moment to circle those criteria that you most value in a job or that you'd like in your work, you'll again gain a better idea of what you need to feel satisfied in your work, regardless of whether you end up taking less pay, advancing at a slower rate, or working in a job that has less prestige or status than what you know you could attain. Remember, as you go through this process, don't feel guilty if you do derive value from your work, be it a sense of independence or a sense of excitement. You have rights. You have the right to seek professional fulfillment. You have the right to lead an intellectually and emotionally satisfying life, and work can help provide that. After you've circled the values that are most important to you, write them down under "Professional Needs" on your bookmark.

CAREER VALUES CARD SORT*

TIME FREEDOM
Have responsibilities I can work at according to my time schedule; no specific working hours required.

INFLUENCE PEOPLE
Be in a position to change attitudes or opinions of other people.

CREATIVE EXPRESSION
Be able to express in writing and in person my ideas concerning the job and how I might improve it; have opportunities for experimentation and innovation.

ARTISTIC CREATIVITY
Engage in creative work in any of several art forms.

LOCATION
Find place to live (town, geographic area) conducive to my lifestyle, learning, and work life.

CREATIVITY (general)
Create new ideas, programs, organized structures, or anything else not following a format developed by others.

RECOGNITION
Get positive feedback and public credit for work well done.

STATUS
Impress or gain the respect of friends, family, and community by the nature and/or level of responsibility of my work.

FRIENDSHIPS
Develop close personal relationships with people as a result of work activity.

JOB TRANQUILITY
Avoid pressure and the rat race in job role and work setting.

CHALLENGING PROBLEMS
Engage continually with complex questions and demanding tasks, troubleshooting and problem solving as core parts of job.

COMPETITION
Engage in activities that pit my abilities against others.

ADVANCEMENT
Be able to get ahead rapidly, gaining opportunities for growth and seniority from work well done.

ADVENTURE
Have work duties that involve frequent risk taking.

CHANGE AND VARIETY
Have work responsibilities frequently changed in content and setting.

WORK UNDER PRESSURE
Work in time-pressured circumstances in which there is little or no margin for error, or with demanding personal relationships.

PHYSICAL CHALLENGE
Have a job that requires bodily strength, speed, dexterity, or agility.

PROFIT, GAIN
Have strong likelihood of accumulating large amounts of money or other material gain through ownership, profit sharing, commissions, merit pay increases, and the like.

AESTHETICS
Be involved in studying or appreciating the beauty of things, ideas, etc.

INTELLECTUAL STATUS
Be regarded as very well informed and a strong theorist, as one acknowledged expert in a given field.

MAKE DECISIONS
Have the power to decide courses of action, policies, etc.; a judgment job.

STEEP LEARNING CURVE
Be presented with new, unique, or difficult tasks to be quickly mastered.

PERSONAL SAFETY
Have a high probability of being safe and healthy at work.

TRADITION
Be involved in work that yields a practical or useful result.

WORK–LIFE BALANCE
A job that allows me adequate time for my family, hobbies, and social activities.

ENVIRONMENT
Work on tasks that have a positive effect on the natural environment.

PRACTICALITY
Be involved in work that yields a practical or useful result.

MORAL FULFILLMENT
Feel that my work is contributing to ideals that I feel are very important.

WORK ON FRONTIERS OF KNOWLEDGE
Work in research and development, generating information and new ideas in the academic, scientific, or business community.

KNOWLEDGE
Engage myself in pursuit of knowledge, truth, and understanding.

HIGH EARNINGS ANTICIPATED
Be able to purchase essentials and the luxuries of life I wish.

FAST PACE
Work in circumstances where there is high-pace activity and work done rapidly.

HELP OTHERS
Be involved in helping people directly, either individually or in small groups.

SECURITY
Be ensured of keeping my job and of receiving a reasonable financial reward.

WORK ALONE
Do projects by myself, without any amount of contact with others.

EXERCISE COMPETENCE
Demonstrate a high degree of proficiency in job skills and knowledge; show above-average effectiveness.

AFFILIATION
Be recognized as a member of a particular organization.

SUPERVISION
Have a job in which I am directly responsible for work done by others.

POWER AND AUTHORITY
Control or partially control the work activities or destinies of others.

EXCITEMENT
Experience a high degree of stimulation or frequent novelty and drama on the job.

DIVERSITY
Work in a setting that includes individuals of diverse religious, racial, and social backgrounds.

WORK WITH OTHERS
Have close working relations with the group; work as a team to reach common goals.

PUBLIC CONTACT
Have a lot of day-to-day contact with people.

STABILITY
Have a work routine and job duties that are largely predictable and not likely to change over a long period of time.

PRECISION WORK
Deal with tasks that have exact specifications or that require careful, accurate attention to detail.

COMMUNITY
Live in a town or city where I can meet my neighbors and become active in local politics or service projects.

HONESTY AND INTEGRITY
Work in a setting in which honesty and integrity are assets.

STRUCTURE AND PREDICTABILITY
Do work with a high level of structure and predictability.

SPIRITUALITY
Work in a setting that is supportive of my spiritual beliefs.

FUN AND HUMOR
Work in a setting in which it is possible (and appropriate) to joke and have fun.

GROUP AND TEAM
Work with a group to obtain team (rather than individual) results.

INDEPENDENCE
Be able to determine nature of work without significant direction from others; not have to follow instructions or conform to regulations.

HELP SOCIETY
Do something to contribute to the betterment of the world.

FAMILY
Ensure that the type of work I do and the hours I work fit with my family responsibilities.

What If?

So what happens if you go through this process and find that you have been compelled to take on a job that does not fulfill these criteria due to financial needs or the demands of your children? Or that quite simply it's unrealistic for you to fulfill all your needs through work? Don't despair. Ask yourself, instead, if there are other areas of your life that can address those needs. If a sense of accomplishment is important to you, can you get some of that sense of accomplishment from another area of your life? Does your work have to be the sole fulfiller of that need? If power is important to you, can you meet some of that need through organization-based work that is more child-friendly in its time commitments?

Anne Ziff, a marriage and family therapist in private practice in Manhattan, New York, and Westport, Connecticut, teaches patients and therapists about the changes in the family system with the introduction of pregnancy and a new baby. She stresses the importance of self-awareness and self-knowledge when trying to define what needs work meets and how to protect yourself and your family when meeting those needs.

> It's important to rely on oneself [to meet one's needs] and not to use a job, or any other external thing or person, as the exclusive vehicle for these. Too often, one partner gets all her or his socializing needs met in the work environment and has little, if anything, left for the other. Or at work you're brilliant and appreciated, so you can be a pain in the neck at home. Or your partner is taciturn, so you go to work and get to be creative and understood and "part of things." And that's just one aspect. Curiosity needs to be yours and from inside you; if you exclusively use work and its intellectual challenges to stimulate yourself, you're dependent on work for this. What about the rest of your hours, not at work? What are you then? And how does this boost your self-

If You Are Going Back to Work Because You've Divorced or Lost a Spouse

You may be compelled to reenter the workforce due to financial needs that stem from a divorce or loss of a spouse. Difficult as that transition may be emotionally, logistically, even physically, a job can bring unanticipated benefits to your life, ranging from a diminished sense of isolation to a greater sense of empowerment. Those benefits can be an integral part of a refocusing in your life, a refocusing that can be healing in itself. "A lot of growth can happen, especially if you let it," says one Mississippi-based mother to three who was a stay-at-home mother for 11.5 years before she divorced. "I've seen a lot of women whose husbands have left them, and they're stuck in the mire—but mire can be a very fertilizing thing."

confidence? If you're aware of yourself as being creative and intellectually curious, and then you get a job outside the home, and you love it because it's stimulating and challenging, you have an excellent mix of your talents being valued and put to use in the workplace.

If given your family's needs, you can't get the job you'd otherwise seek, you won't have failed. You simply will have taken a pragmatic and often necessary approach to managing your personal and professional life, an approach taken by many mothers with family-friendly work.

Determining Your Personal Needs

Don't believe that you can fulfill those personal needs outside work? Well, you can, but making that change successfully will require a refocusing of your mind, a renewed sense of "self-awareness," that transcendent vision I mentioned previously. It will require you to think outside the box, to devote energy to interests that in past years have waned. Take Maggie. Having trained in a highly regarded retail program and owned her own custom-designed swimwear shop, she is now an executive recruiter in retail precisely because, she says, it affords her the opportunity to work part-time from home, make a sizable income, draw on an existing skill set, and stay connected to an industry that she knew well. But executive recruiting is not who she is.

> *Being an executive recruiter does not particularly stimulate or challenge me intellectually. It also doesn't fulfill some creative needs I have. [But] I wouldn't do it any other way right now, because my kids are my priority. So, to fill the lack of intellectual stimulation, I read voraciously, and to fill the gap on the creative front, I take guitar lessons once a week.*

Kristi, the woman you met earlier in this book who runs that needlepoint shop, has a similar perspective to her work. While it doesn't provide her with the same financial or intellectual satisfaction that she once enjoyed professionally, her work arrangement does answer other needs: use of management skills, income, and a job that gives her the opportunity to interact with others. And it has brought with it benefits she didn't expect. Since taking over the business, she has taken an ailing community association and transformed it into a high-profile forum for women's concerns, creating a large and impressive network of her own. And at the same time, she's still made her business a small success, proving she can use the business acumen she applied to a large corporation on the small scale of a retail shop.

Every woman will not feel she has the time to devote to pursuing interests outside work. But those interests do not have to take large time slots of your life. You can satisfy those interests in small ways, such as setting aside 15 minutes at night to read before you go to bed and thus take yourself out of a life dominated by work and kids. You

IF YOU HAVE A PARTNER

Don't forget to create time with your partner. Your relationship needs energy put toward it too. As more mothers work, the dynamics of family life are changing. New pressures are being introduced; old ones are being relieved. Be sure you both make conscious efforts to communicate your needs to each other. Find the arrangement that works best for you as a couple. Come to an agreement as to how you are delegating child care and other domestic responsibilities. Don't let resentments build up. Support one another, and don't forget to have fun. Your children will be better off for it.

IF YOU ARE A SINGLE MOTHER

You too need time for yourself. You also need adult stimulation and companionship, whether that's romance or a great friendship. If finding a partner is important to you, don't feel guilty for taking time off from the kids to go on a date or enjoy adult company. Don't be afraid to ask for support from friends and family. Your emotional well-being directly affects that of your kids. Stay true to yourself.

can, like Maggie, take one lesson a week to learn something new. But if you are compelled to take a job that does not fulfill all your personal or professional needs, you'll need to understand what it does bring and what it does not and then seek out what's missing in other areas of your life. You'll need to ask yourself where you can satisfy needs in your life outside work. Is it in a place of worship, a volunteer group, or a playgroup with your kids? You need to eke out time toward what's important to you, whether dating, exercising, a spouse, or friends. Says a mother who runs her own advertising business four days per week and sets clear office hours for herself: "It is vital to have something for yourself, be it paid work or some sort of interest. Giving time to yourself is not depriving your child. You need balance!"

So take a moment to consider what you'd like to carve out time for, and think about the frequency you can expect to do that. Then write it down under the heading "Personal Needs" on your bookmark.

Be Realistic with Your Time

As you do this, don't fall into the trap of creating unrealistic expectations for yourself as a parent, professional, or a spouse. To create time for yourself, be willing to let some things go and to cut yourself some slack as to when you get the less important chores done. Your home, for example, doesn't have to be immaculate. Says Anne Wilson Schaef in her best-selling book *Meditations for Women Who Do Too Much:* "One of the comforting qualities about housework is that it is always there."[1] Rest assured, even those women who appear to have it all figured out with satisfying work and "extremely" family-friendly jobs can't figure out how to get all the chores done. Their mothers may have had aspirations to be Julia Child but they know that striving to be Martha Stewart is not realistic. "I'm not suggesting I've got it all figured out," one woman with family-friendly work told me. "Last night I was roaming the supermarket aisles at 10:30 at night."

"My biggest challenge is housecleaning," says another woman, a single mom from South Dakota with one teenage son and a job in a government research center as a chemistry lab technician. "I wish I could say I've found a way to make it easy, but I haven't. I just stopped setting such high standards for myself. When my son is out of the house, he won't remember whether or not I dusted every week, but he will remember the games I attended or other important times we spent together. Our house is clean enough to be healthy, but it wouldn't be featured in a Windex commercial. And that's just fine with me and my son."

Remember what's most important in your life and focus your energy toward that. Ask yourself, "When I look back at my life in 25 years, will I have any regrets?"

Learn to accept doing what you can, getting help for other things, and letting go of the rest. For doing chores, Anne Ziff tells patients with partners to do the following:

If You or a Member of Your Family Just Can't Manage

Sometimes people feel overwhelmed with their life situations and are unable to make any decisions with confidence. Be aware that depression and other emotional problems are very common, and that state-of-the-art treatment can work wonders. If this description fits you, talk with your family doctor. Note, too, that the stresses of work life and home life readily create conflicts in marital relationships; couples counseling may straighten out the lines of communication to everyone's benefit. And, finally, children and teenagers themselves often suffer from symptoms of emotional problems. Your pediatrician can make a referral for an evaluation by a child psychiatrist or other appropriately trained professional.

I approach this with index cards and make it a game. I ask my clients to call out absolutely every chore that requires attention in the home on a daily, weekly, monthly, annual basis. Each goes on a card. I tell them to spread all the cards on a flat surface, and say, "On your mark, get set, go," then each should grab the tasks they are happy to do. When they both stop, I ask them to see what tasks are left. Each should ask, "Are there others I'd be willing to take on?" Then, with the leftover cards, ask, "Who can we hire to do these? Can we afford to do that?" and deal realistically and accordingly.

Last, always bear in mind things will change. Your children will grow up. Your house one day will be empty of children and as clean as you'd like it to be. Enjoy what you have. Take pleasure in the reason behind the trade-offs you make. Kelsey, a mother of two, labored over her decision to, as she calls it, temporarily "trade-down" her career as an investment banker to become "a glorified sales assistant at a large stock brokerage for a year to keep my licenses intact." But now she's again in a very senior position as director of operations for a high-tech start-up in Washington. "I wanted to be there for my daughter," she says of her former position at the stock brokerage. "I do not regret that decision. Financially, the pay was dismally pale in comparison, but I only had to take one business trip that year, and I got to be very involved in my little girl's world. Being with her every day was priceless."

Exercise

Get out that bookmark again. If you haven't done so already, go back to those values you circled (on pp. 36–37) and list them under "Professional Needs." Also list those values you identified in the exercise put together by Kathleen Kreis. If you haven't done so already, write down what you'd like in the way of personal time, whether it be time to exercise each week, meals shared with your spouse, a night out with friends, or to be able to go on dates. Keep this bookmark with you as you go to the next chapter.

Real Mother Recap

Remember that you have needs as a woman. If working makes you happier, you'll be a happier mom. Whatever you do, don't apologize for the route you choose. Just take the time to identify the needs of you and your family. Then take pride in the decisions you make, knowing that those decisions are based on the needs that you and your family face.

If you need more help: Richard Knowdell's *Career Values Card Sort Planning Kit* is a good resource. Call 408-441-9100 or visit his Web site to find out more (www.careertrainer.com). If you need more information on juggling work and home than these chapters provide, pick up a copy of the magazine *Working Mother* or visit Working Moms Refuge at www.momsrefuge.com.

4

Know What You Must Earn

I would tell a single mom in that situation that I was in to be brutally honest, to work out a budget. Budgets are like rules, not to be broken. If you can afford it, get an accountant. Getting a few good people around you is important. So is investing in an asset, like a house.

—MOLLY

MOLLY

"*I thought that I was Murphy Brown,*" says 51-year-old Molly on how she felt at 34, pregnant, single, and working as editor-in-chief at a start-up cooking magazine. But 10 months after giving birth to Dede, her self-perception radically changed.

"*I was the first person there to have a baby. My boss couldn't understand why I wouldn't stay until 10 o'clock at night,*" she says. "*After having stayed home one day to care for Dede, who was running a temperature of 102 degrees, I found my boss coming to my house to tell me that I was very good at my job but that he was getting an ulcer.*" That was it. He fired her there and then.

"*Life is what happens while you're planning for it to happen,*" says Molly in looking back at how she managed to single-handedly raise one child while working as a self-employed writer from *home. She's matter-of-fact, casually dressed, the sort of person you could share a pot of coffee with.*

"I don't remember panicking at being able to raise a child. I began actively looking for a job, freelancing at the same time. Then four months later, I realized I could earn money and have a flexible schedule." So she stopped looking for permanent employment and went freelance full-time.

Since then, Molly—still a single mother to her 19-year-old daughter, who started Stanford last fall—has edited numerous cookbooks, written hundreds of food-related articles, and consulted for a number of organizations on food-related topics. She founded the Women's Culinary Alliance in her town and is, she readily concedes, very good at networking. Very important if you want to freelance, she says.

In fact, Molly shares many traits with some of the higher-paid women featured in this book. She has a strong network, marketable skills, and a solid knowledge base—assets that she's well aware bring value to her and to her clients. "I've always had confidence in my ability to make money," she says, "I approach my freelance job as a business."

That approach has paid off. Molly now earns an annual income of anywhere between $70,000 and $100,000 a year. Not bad for someone who started her career at $100 a week.

Still, she makes trade-offs. She gets no employer-sponsored benefits. Not every job is ideal. She doesn't use all her skills or knowledge in every project she undertakes. And she often defers to management less experienced than herself. But these are realities she accepts as necessary in getting the flexibility and autonomy she seeks. These are trade-offs that, after 18 years, she happily makes.

Budget? Not that Molly ever wrote one down. She did draw a will when her child was born. She then got life insurance and an agent to help her find and negotiate work. And when she started to make enough money to cover more than basic living costs, she hired an accountant who told her to open an IRA. When her daughter was 9 or 10, Molly even started saving for college tuition by setting up an investment account, which has grown over the years. Still, she concedes, "I'm not a good money person."

Not a good money person? Molly has managed to save for every major life event, employing an accountant to help. While she may not adhere to a written budget, she is, she attests, fiscally conservative by nature, living by a budget in her head. "I always know how much money I have and where," she states. In other words, Molly knows exactly what she has to earn to meet her saving objectives and the daily living expenses that being a single mother demands. That knowledge helps her determine what job best meets her needs. Why? Because most of us do, after all, work above all to get paid.

"But come on. You can't really make money with family-friendly work," a friend told me in reference to this book.

Responses from my survey suggest the contrary, friend. Women who answered my survey live throughout the United States, from the small town in Connecticut where I live to Walnut Creek, California. These women work in a wide range of jobs: teaching, advertising, nursing, marketing, publishing, finance, sales, real estate, energy, law, nonprofit work, manufacturing—you name it. But for the most part, the respondents who call their work "very" or "extremely" family-friendly are not toiling away with no income to show for it. The average respondent in my survey who says she holds a family-friendly job earns between $50,000 and $100,000 a year. Some may earn less than what they consider their earning potential, but not all bear a financial cost for family-friendly work. One respondent who used to work in the philanthropic division of a large bank practically tripled her pay when she set out on her own to do philanthropic consulting from home (read: own boss, no commute, home office, and flexible hours—in other words, extremely family-friendly work).

But most family-friendly arrangements do come at a price, particularly for those with few relevant skills, education, or experience
on which they can trade. Most of the women in my survey who say
they have "extremely" or "very" family-friendly work also have a
college education; some even have graduate degrees.

Exceptions exist. Take the experience of one survey respondent,
a chemical operator at a plant in Virginia. She works 12-hour shifts
but has managed to band together with colleagues to trade hours so
that they all can better accommodate family demands, despite the
opposition from other departments in the plant. "Other departments took issue, saying we shouldn't be allowed to do it," remarks
this mother of three. "But we are so much happier now knowing
that when we need a day off we can get it." Still, among the lowest
paid, such stories are few and far between. Says one full-time administrative assistant, a single mother to five kids in Tennessee: "I
can't even bring in a genuine doctor's excuse when one of my children are sick without feeling there could be consequences."

The reality is that the more value you bring (in the form of relevant skills, experience, education, or knowledge), the more you are
worth to an employer. The more you are worth, the more the employer may be willing to meet your needs and the more likely you
are to be able to take less pay—if need be—to get what you want. So
ask yourself, if you were to change your work arrangement, how
much would you need to make? The operative word here is *need*.
Not *deserve*. Not *want*. But *need*.

How to Figure That Out

Get out your pencil, recommends Jay Kansky, an independent financial adviser. Or, as Molly suggests at the beginning of this chapter, sit down and work out a budget. "Begin by carrying a list with
you wherever you go. Record your expenses daily. Write down

everything you spend for three months. Multiply it by four and then you'll know how much you need to make on a yearly basis to get by," says Kansky. That list should include all your bills—from credit cards to mortgage payments—as well as incidental costs, such as that morning cup of coffee. Now add to that sum your regular contributions for savings-related costs, such as retirement, college education, and life insurance. Make sure you've set aside enough for some sort of savings, even it it's only a small kitty for retirement. "Try to be consistent in your contributions to [your savings] plans," advises Kansky. "If it gets to the point where it's too expensive to save, try to cut back on your spending." Sit with your spouse or partner if you have one, or someone you trust if you don't, and determine how much you need to be earning to cover your expenses and how much you need to contribute to savings and insurance.

Retirement Savings

As you go through the process of estimating what you need to earn, err on the conservative, especially concerning retirement savings. The reason is that as a woman, you are statistically more vulnerable to financial hardship. Women, on average, earn some 76¢ for every dollar a man earns—leaving them with lower retirement savings and smaller security checks later on.[1] Of course, smaller retirement savings would be fine if you could guarantee that you would benefit equally from a partner's pay down the line. But as strong as your relationship might be—as much as that eyes-only-for-you spouse of yours might tell you that you are the axis of his world, odds are that you will end up on your own in later life. Women tend to outlive men by more than 5 years.[2] And not all of them are entitled to their spouse's retirement package. Moreover, the number of older divorced women—in their late 50s to 60s—has now outnumbered widows.[3] Due to their divorce settlements, many of these women are

Women and Retirement

Women are not as bad off as they once were. Many employers once offered defined benefit plans that carried 5-year vesting periods. And looking at median years of tenure over the last 20 years, women in the 35 to 44 age bracket suffered disproportionately because they, unlike men in the same age bracket, consistently remained with an employer for less than 5 years. Fortunately, however, employers now are more inclined to offer some sort of contribution plan or "cash balance" plan by which employees can start setting money aside almost immediately, so women who stay with their employer fewer than 5 years aren't excluded from accumulating retirement savings. And that's undoubtedly a good thing because a woman's average tenure during those child-rearing years of 35 to 54 is still significantly behind a man's.* Still, shorter tenures can make it harder to climb the ranks, leading to fewer salary advances down the line. In fact, even with the less onerous retirement savings plans, the ratio of women's to men's defined contribution plan accumulations was still only 44 percent in 1998.† That means women didn't have half of what men had stored away through their employer plans.

*Bureau of Census for the Bureau of Labor Statistics, *Employee Tenure Survey, 2002* [Taken from supplemental questions of the *Current Population Survey, 2002*] (Washington, DC: U.S. Department of Labor, 2002). Available at www.bls.gov/news.release/tenure.nr0.htm; accessed on March 30, 2003.

†The percentage of employed women with a pension or retirement plan at their current job was 45%, compared to 52% for employed men, and the ratio of women's to men's defined contribution plan accumulations was only 44% in 1998. Employee Benefit Research Institute, "Women and Pensions: A Decade of Progress?" [Issue Brief 227] (Washington, DC: Employee Benefit Research Institute, November 2000).

not entitled to their ex-husband's pension or savings plans. They often have little to nothing in the way of a pension or retirement savings, because they moved out of the workforce to rear children.

Their present working income is their pension; they're getting little retirement income any other way.

Don't believe this scenario could happen to you? Meet Georgina, a mother to five children. I came across this soft-spoken, 65-year-old supplies manager at a small software company. She told me in hushed tones as she scuttled around the office that she never thought she would find herself living with her child and looking forward to what little relief social security benefits might bring. Her husband divorced her more than a decade earlier, after she had spent about 10 years of her life working part-time in teaching and the next 15 years working from home as an officer manager for her husband's landscaping company. "You can't see what's going to happen," she says of her life. The way her divorce left her financially is too painful to discuss. So much for those relaxed, post-child-rearing, retirement years.

These statistics aren't meant to get you down. Instead, use this knowledge to sit your still young-*ish* bottom down and gain a clear understanding of your financial situation. Then be sure you take that into account as you figure out what you would need to earn if you change your work situation. If you're lucky enough to have a partner who meets your financial needs, do what you can together to ensure that your financial needs will be met down the line.

Does Your Nine-Year-Old *Really* Need $200 Sneakers and a Cell Phone?

When you determine your expenses, be honest with yourself about what you really need to earn. Yes, savings and insurance are important, but look hard at your daily and one-off expenses as well. Ask yourself if your children really need the latest deluxe swing-set or would they benefit more from a little more of your time and a little less expendable income? Naomi Drew, a conflict resolution specialist and parenting expert who recently wrote *Peaceful Parents, Peaceful Kids: Practical Ways to Create a Calm and Happy Home*[4] (doesn't that sound nice?) and is herself a veteran mother, often finds herself counseling parents who believe their children are benefiting from a wide range of toys and amusements when a little more concentrated time would serve the children better. Income is vital, but so is perspective.

Look at what one mother who calls her job "not-at-all" family-friendly writes:

> *I work to give my children things that my parents couldn't provide.*
> *They know that the reason I work so hard is to provide private school,*
> *nice vacations, karate lessons, acting classes, and experiences that*
> *their friends have. They're used to it. But I have to work so hard and*
> *sometimes I wonder if it's worth it.*

Makes you think about your own situation, doesn't it? It sure made me think about my own. So think about how much you truly need to earn.

Wealth Is in the Eye of the Beholder

When I began writing this book, the immediate reaction of so many women was that a job that meets your family's needs is fine for someone who can rely on her spouse's income, but it's altogether different for someone who has to support herself. *(Ouch!)* But in fact, the perceived financial needs of women I interviewed for this book by no means coincided with the amount of income that a partner, spouse, or absent father did or did not make. It often came down to what a woman *thought* she did or didn't need to earn. Take Kristi, the owner of that small needlepoint shop. She says the primary reason that she returned to work after the birth of her second child was finances. So she quickly returned to her long commute and high-paying city job. Whereas Lea, an immigrant mother of one, returned to the labor force one year after the birth of her child, *not* for the money but for the sense of personal empowerment and security that work provided. Lea's husband eked out only a modest living as an employee of a landscaping company, whereas Kristi lived in an affluent suburb with a husband who worked in a much higher-paying position. That is not to say that Kristi might not have needed the income. Perhaps Kristi's lifestyle was more expensive, her mortgage higher, her debts larger, and her desire for financial security greater. Regardless, vantage point clearly comes into play when defining *need*.

So don't limit yourself by saying "I work these long hours simply because we need the income." Ascertain whether that's in fact truth for you. Many people derive more out of work than pay. Intellectual challenge, social interaction, and a sense of empowerment are among them. That's okay. But if you can establish what you need to earn first, you may find that more options exist than you previously thought. You may be able to fulfill that need for intellectual challenge through work that you previously ruled out because it did not pay as much. Or you may finally be able to find the courage to alter the arrangement you currently have. Take the time to think about how much you need to earn. And once you've done that, remember the following parable.

A successful businesswoman went to a beach and found a fisherwoman bringing in a day's catch at 3:00. She watched the woman slowly walking ashore and then, as the fisherwoman sat down to rest and look out at the vast sea, the businesswoman approached her.

"Good day fishing?" the businesswoman asked.

"Yes," said the fisherwoman. "The fish were biting and I've got a good day's worth of pay here."

"You'd probably increase that if you go out again this afternoon as well," the businesswoman remarked.

The fisherwoman looked perplexed. "No, it's afternoon now, and I was out at daybreak. I'll take the rest of the day off," she said.

The businesswoman looked at the catch and thought for a moment. "You know, if you worked longer days, you could catch far more. Better yet, you could hire some people to do it for you and free your own time up to concentrate on your business."

"Why would I want to do that?" the fisherwoman asked.

"Well, then you could spend time getting a better price for your catch and distribute it to the right places where fresh fish like yours would be in high demand. You even could move into town, get a proper office. You'd earn much more."

"Why would I want do that?" the fisherwoman asked, looking even more perplexed.

"Well, then you could retire one day, out to a place like this, on the ocean, in a small seaside cottage, and really enjoy life. You could do what you love, perhaps fish in the mornings then be home in the late afternoon."

"Yes," said the fisherwoman. "I see." And she smiled at the businesswoman, collected her catch and headed home for the late afternoon.

Exercise

Now, if you're feeling so inclined, get out the bookmark again. Next to "Income Needs," write down the minimum that *you*—not your spouse or partner—need to earn based on your annual expenses. Be sure to factor in savings- and insurance-related costs as well as expenses that are *not* covered by your spouse's or partner's income. It's important to take into consideration the income of a spouse or partner because you need not duplicate efforts. Viewing your earnings in this way will give you a better bare-bones assessment of what compensation you absolutely need. As you go through this process, be honest with yourself, basing your figure on *need* not *want*. You may end up earning more than the figure you write down, but this base figure is meant to give you a picture of the flexibility you do or don't have in the type of employment you seek by determining the remuneration it must bring.

Real Mother Recap

So, you've done it, completed another part of Step One. But in case you've already forgotten what you read, the class notes read something like this: Take the time to figure out what you need to make, being honest with yourself and erring on the side of conservatism, because women often have it tougher in later life. Give the right weight to your financial needs when determining what you're willing to give and give up in your professional life. Don't be ashamed if you derive satisfaction from earning, but don't let your income determine your sense of personal worth. Remember, the harder job is the one for which you are not paid.

If you need more help understanding the complexities of personal finance, two useful Web sites are The Motley Fool (www.fool.com) and Kiplinger Online (www.kiplinger.com).

5

Understand How Employer-Sponsored Benefits May Help

If I go to work for a company, I want a decent package of benefits.
—KATHY

KATHY

As we talk on the phone, Kathy, mother to two, tells me she's wrapping her legs around the chair. We're talking about something that is leaving her feeling anxious—her job, or more specifically, her lack of one.

Six months ago, Kathy's husband, Jake, went back to school so that he could start his own business in landscape design. He always had a desire to do that work, but with a toddler and a baby, he had been reluctant to turn his back on the security of a well-paying job. When his company downsized, Kathy encouraged him to take a chance.

His business is now doing relatively well, given the fact that he is new to the field. He is busy, not always doing the work that he likes, but checks are starting to roll in. He's got health care for himself and his family, but he has to pay a lot for his insurance be-

cause of his severe allergies. They haven't got life and dental in-surance. Nor is Jake making enough money to invest in any form of retirement fund. Paying the mortgage and meeting the expenses of daily life is challenging enough.

"Jake tells me, 'You're over-focusing on benefits.' But I'd like to know there was something behind us. I'd like some security."

So Kathy is looking for a job. Having worked in recruiting and research in the field of fine arts, Kathy suspects she'll end up using those same skills again, though perhaps in a different field. She's trying not to limit herself, but her family-friendly options in the short term are limited in some respects.

Being a school guidance counselor, for example, appeals to her. Such a position would provide a schedule that would coincide with her children's when they attend school. The problem is that she thinks to get such a job, she would have to go back to school. She's going to talk to the local university and a local school to ascertain how much the appropriate schooling will cost, how long it will take, and the prospects for someone like her after she got the qualification the university program gives. But she clearly has her doubts. "All that takes at least a year, and it's expensive. We'd have to think long and hard about that."

In the meantime, she's going to research jobs in the human resources departments of nearby businesses. In the end, economics will be a driving factor in determining what's right. Yes, a job at a company that provides eight-hour days, flexible scheduling and a four-day workweek would be ideal. But the benefits are what she needs most.

"I want the security," she stresses. "At home, waiting for the income to start appearing is nerve-wracking. And if I could get a better plan for Jake's health care, I'd feel a lot better."

I know. It's not quite as simple as that. You can't sit down, write down your expenses, and say "That's what I need to earn."

Or maybe you can.

Maybe the financial side of the equation is as simple as that. Maybe you have a spouse or a partner who is happily employed and whose compensation adequately covers expenses, savings, and insurance costs and provides a small cushion for your family's comfort as well, leaving you to do whatever kind of work in whatever kind of arrangement you like. But if you don't have a partner, or if your partner is self-employed or has minimal benefits, that may not be the case. Getting access to employer-sponsored benefits—which can boost your compensation package by thousands—may be important. Those benefits are why Kate, a mother to three whose husband is a self-employed builder, works for a large employer, despite the long hours event marketing demands. "One entrepreneur in the family is enough. I have a steady paycheck. I get benefits," she says. They are also part of the reason that Monica, the director of career services at a university in Nevada, works for her employer who provides full coverage for her entire family, invests money for her family's education, and will send her children to college for free. "But you also don't make what you make in Corporate America," she reminds me, in case I lapse (which, admittedly, after three children, I often do. But let's face it, before them I probably did too.) Some women, such as Molly from Chapter 4, choose to be self-employed and carry the added costs of insurance and savings. She, after all, has had self-employed status since her daughter was less than a year old. Based on your income needs and comfort levels, only you can decide whether you need employer-sponsored benefits.

But if you do decide you need or want employer-sponsored benefits, you also have to be realistic about what you can get. The most common, for example, are some forms of health, life, and dental insurance as well as some form of retirement plan.[1] For the most part, your chances of getting these and other benefits increase if you choose to work at a larger employer rather than a small one. It's no coincidence, by the way, that these common benefits are the ones that can most affect your bottom line.

- **Health insurance:** Most companies, particularly larger ones, now offer some form of health insurance. Because groups rates are usually less than individual rates, you're probably better off getting this through an employer than paying for your own insurance or for you and your family's.

- **Dental insurance:** Dental insurance is very common among employers now, and more common among larger employers.

- **Life insurance:** Life insurance gives your dependents something to live on should you die. If you've got kids, you need this. Your employer, particularly if it's large, may provide it.

- **Disability insurance:** The Social Security Administration says "Studies show that a 20-year-old worker has a 3 in 10 chance of becoming disabled before reaching retirement age."* Social Security can help, but probably not enough, particularly if you're a single mom who's been dipping in and out of the workforce. Private disability insurance tends to be more expensive than group, so you're better off getting it through an employer or group association, like an alumni group. Again, this type of insurance is more popular among larger employers than small.

- **Retirement planning:** Experts say you'll need to live on 60% to 85% of your preretirement salary during retirement. Many employers offer some sort of retirement plan, 401(k)s being the most popular. As I mentioned earlier, defined benefit plans, based on the length of service, are less common these days. Instead, there are contribution plans or cash balance plans in which deposits are made annually and typically vest immediately or within one year. (Where do your Social Security benefits stand? Visit www.ssa.gov for a benefits estimate or call 800-772-1213.)

- **Group purchasing:** Group purchasing is when an employer offers a discount program for employees. Auto insurance and group homeowners insurance are among them. Group purchasing is not as common as other benefits.

- **General financial planning:** More companies are offering financial planning assistance and education. But still, they're not in the majority. If your employer does not provide assistance and you want professional advice, you may seek the advice of a personal financial adviser. If you do, make sure your adviser is reputable and preferably recommended through someone you respect. The same holds true for insurance agents and stock brokers. If you've got money to invest, think about joining an investment club. The National Association of Investors Corporation (NAIC) reports that its membership is increasingly female.† Investment clubs can provide mentorship, and women who will support you in your quest to learn more about investing. Ask around for a group near you or visit the Web site of National Association of Investors Corporation (www.better-investing.org).

- **Children's education:** You probably won't get help here from your employer, but you'd be wise to set aside some money nonetheless. Many states can help you finance your child's college education through state-run college savings plans or prepaid tuition plans. Contact the College Savings Plans Network details (877-277-6496 or www.collegesavings.org). Also look into education-geared savings accounts, among them education IRAs, which allow you to deposit money in your child's name, and uniform gifts to a minor's account.

- **Adoption assistance:** Many employers have some sort of adoption assistance though many are capped between $2,500 and $4,000. The government allows for a credit on tax returns when income is under a certain level.

- **Tuition reimbursement:** Many employers have some form of tuition reimbursement for either job-related training courses or career-related enrichment. This can be a good benefit for a woman who might be working simply to make ends meet but could clearly benefit from getting further qualification down the line.

---

*Social Security Administration, *Social Security Disability Benefits*, SSA Publication No. 05-10029 (Washington, DC: Social Security Administration, February 2003). Available at www.ssa.gov/pubs/10029.html: accessed on: April 4, 2003.

†The following are the percentages of participating female investment clubs in the NAIC Annual Value Line Investment Survey:

1995 40.7%

1996 40.8%

1997 46.6%

1998 50.2%

1999 54.4%

2000 58.2%

National Association of Investors Corporation, *Value Line Investment Club Performance Surveys* (sponsored by Value Line Inc., 1995, 1996, 1997, 1998, 1999, and 2000).

Factor In the Cost of Child Care

Bear in mind too that the child-care assistance you are likely to receive from your employer probably won't dramatically affect your bottom line, but it can help. Yes, many employers now offer some kind of child-care assistance, the most common being "flexible" or "dependent-care" spending accounts (capped, at this writing, at $5,000) that allow you to deduct from your pretax income and thereby lower taxable earnings. But you still have to pay for that care, even if it costs you less. Remember, too, that you can get help from Uncle Sam as well through a child-care tax credit. Talk to an accountant for details, or contact the Internal Revenue Service (IRS).

Remember too that other parents are a good source of information when it comes to child-care issues; many are dealing with some

How Your Employer May Help You Save on Child Care

• **"Flexible" or "dependent-care" spending accounts:** Deduct the costs of child care from your pretax income. That, in turn, lowers your taxable earnings. This is the child-care program that employers most commonly offer, according to work/life benefit surveys.

• **Resource and referral services:** This benefit is second on the list of most commonly offered child-care benefits that employers offer. Here, the employer has done a lot of the legwork for you in terms of finding someone to help you get the right child care. But you'll still have to evaluate what's right for you and what you can afford.

• **Sick/emergency child-care program:** Policies vary. Check out what your employer has and whether it's affordable.

• **Child-care centers:** Don't bank on this. Still relatively few major employers offer these, which may be on site or off, subsidized or not. And sometimes they're located at headquarters only and still prohibitively expensive for those on minimum or low wage. Be sure that you can afford it, the center has space for your child, the hours match your own, and it's good quality before you get excited about signing on.

• **Employer-arranged discounts with local child care:** About as common as employer-sponsored child-care centers. Again, be sure you're happy with the child care before you sign on and make sure it's affordable.

• **Other less common programs:** Before/after-school care, school holiday programs, camp programs, lactation rooms, consultants, and voucher programs.

of the same issues you face. One human resources (HR) person to whom I spoke says that linking up parents who face similar challenges is one of the most effective ways that employees at her or-

Child-Care Options*

• **Parental care:** Stay-at-home mother, stay-at-home father, shared care (alternating schedules with partner through shift work, part-time schedules, at-home work, or flexible hours). Many experts recommend parental care first, particularly in the early years. But parental care exclusively is not viable or desirable for many families. That's okay. What you want, above all, is quality care. *Cost:* $0.00, expect loss of income

• **Relative care:** Care provided by an individual related to the child. It's hard to find much research on the effects of relative care. But most experts agree that quality comes first. Be sure your child's caregiver is loving and attentive. *Cost:* depends on particular arrangement

• **Child-care centers:** Care provided in nonresidential facilities, usually for 13 or more children. Again, quality is key. Experts recommend that you seek out qualified, experienced caregivers, low teacher-to-child ratios, and other criteria listed in "Five Things You Can Do About Child Care" (on pp. 65–66). According to the National Institute of Child Health and Human Development (NICHD), a stimulating and well-organized setting can help children in the development of language and school readiness, as well as lead to fewer behavioral problems than children in centers with poor professional standards. *Cost:* $4,000–$10,000 per child

• **Family child-care providers:** Care provided in a private residence other than the child's home. This option can be desirable because groups are often small, kids usually have a consistent caregiver, and they are sometimes cheaper than child-care centers. But family child-care providers are sometimes less professional than child-care centers. Be sure yours is top quality. *Cost:* $4,000–$10,000 per child

• **In-home caregivers:** Care provided within the child's home by a person other than a parent or relative. Many consider the one-on-one care ideal; but again, you want a nanny who is experienced, reliable, and understands your child's needs.

Cost: $13,000–$35,000

• **Care-giving co-ops:** Newly emerging type of care in which parents time-share responsibility of caring for the children.

Cost: depends on specific arrangement

*National Institute of Child Health and Human Development, *Study of Early Child Care.* (American Journal of Public Health, July 1999)

ganization get advice when it comes to managing children and work. Your HR professional may also be able to give you some direction through resource and referral agencies. If you are at a loss, you'll need more resources than this book. To get you thinking about this decision as it relates to your financial needs, however, I've listed options and their estimated yearly costs in the box "Child-Care Options."

As you think about these issues, bear in mind what one mother told me: How well a job works depends largely on how you feel about your child care. So if a family-friendly arrangement requires a new or altered form of child care—because of either a shift in the hours you work or a change in pay—you'll want to make sure that you are happy with the care that your children are getting. If your arrangement puts you in a situation in which you are compelled to make use of child care that you feel is inadequate, your job is *not* family-friendly. Or to put this whole child-care consideration into Ellen's words, the woman mentioned in Chapter 1, "Make sure what you're doing is worth what you'll have to arrange. Sometimes it's very clear—we need the money. Other times, you may be better off if you take part-time or evening work. Try to look at your decision objectively."

Five Things You Can Do About Child Care

As you think about what child-care arrangement is right for your children, take the time to assess the quality of the care your child will be receiving. Again and again, research suggests that quality matters—a lot. The following guidelines are recommended by the Child Care Action Campaign.*

LOOK

Visit several homes or centers. Look for a safe environment with toys, books and materials within a child's reach. Do the teachers enjoy talking and playing with children? Are infants able to crawl and explore safely? Do providers devote time to one-on-one activities with infants and toddlers, to reading to children, and to frequent conversation?

LISTEN

Do the children sound happy and involved? Do they converse easily with each other and with caregivers? Do caregivers speak in cheerful and patient tones? Too much noise may signal a lack of control; too much quiet may mean not enough activity. Is TV used as a substitute for more stimulating activities?

COUNT

Count the children in the group, and the number of staff members caring for them. For each adult, there should be no more than: 3 to 4 infants or toddlers; 4 to 6 two-year-olds; 7 to 8 three-year-olds; 8 to 9 four-year-olds; 8 to 10 five-year-olds.

ASK

What is the background and experience of all staff? Providers trained in child-care development are more likely to be able to meet your child's individual needs. Ask about staff turnover. Find out if family providers are licensed, and if the center or home is accredited by a professional organization.

CHECK

Talk to other parents who have used the center or home. Go to www. childcareaware.org [or call 800-424-4226] to find the child-care resource and

referral agency nearest you. (They can also help you navigate financial assistance.) Even after you start using child care, continue to drop in and check it out
for quality.

*Child Care Action Campaign, *Five Things You Can Do About Child Care* (2001). Available
    at: www.childcareaction.org/staction.html; accessed on: March 15, 2003.

A Few Other Benefits to Consider

Of course, the number of work/life benefits that an employer may
offer extends far beyond child care. Eldercare assistance is becoming
more popular, though still relatively uncommon. The same holds
true for adoption assistance. As you get to the stage at which you are
assessing your prospective employer, you'll also want to consider
other specific policies that fall under work/life policies, such as
leave. But even maternity leave is legislated in some cases to provide
only 12 weeks of *unpaid* leave. Paid leave is still relatively rare. Likewise, sick leave, leave to care for a sick child, and holiday leave are all
important, but they won't—given how they are currently offered to
most people—help you much financially. Some companies even provide paid time off for volunteering, a real asset for mothers who
want time to volunteer at their children's school.

If Money Is Tight

If, however, you are a mother who needs to earn every dime she can,
you probably want to find an arrangement in which you are eligible
for as many financial benefits as you can get. In fact, the average

If You're a Low-Income Mother

HEALTH CARE

Despite the fact that many employers do offer health insurance, many people still have no health insurance. Reasons for lack of insurance vary from employers not carrying it, long waiting periods for enrollment, and unaffordable programs. That and other factors, such as unemployment, mean that millions of children in the United States go without health insurance. If your children are among them, contact the Children's Defense Fund at www.childrensdefense.org or call your state program at 877-KIDS-NOW to see what programs your children qualify for. They may qualify for the Children's Health Insurance Program or Medicaid. Find out.

CHILD CARE

Research shows that quality child care—particularly in the early years—is key to a child's development. Yet for many, it's unaffordable. Full-day child care in centers often costs between $4,000 and $10,000 or even higher per child per year. Family child care can cost only marginally less. Even part-time care for school-age children (before/after school and holidays) can cost thousands.* Yet more than one out of four families with young children earns less than $25,000 a year.† Some initiatives, like Head Start, have been established to help. Through Child Care Aware and a Child Care Resource and Referral agency (CCR&R), you can find information on locating child care and child-care resources in your area. Visit www.childcareaware.org and type in your zip code to locate a CCR&R branch in your area, or call 800-424-2246.

*Karen Schulman, *Issue Brief: The High Cost of Child Care Puts Quality Care Out of Reach for Many Families* (Washington, DC: Children's Defense Fund, 2000). Available at www. childrensdefense.org/pdf; accessed on: March 14, 2003.

†U.S. Census Bureau, *Money Income in the United States: 1999* [Current Population Reports, P60–209] (Washington, DC: U.S. Government Printing Office, 2000), cited in *Child Care Basics* (Children's Defense Fund, April 2001). Available at www.childrensdefense.org/cc_ facts.htm; accessed on March 14, 2003.

The Lowdown on Leave

• Determine whether or not you are eligible to take time off under the federal Family and Medical Leave Act (FMLA): The FMLA allows eligible workers to take up to 12 weeks of unpaid leave to care for newborn or adopted children, to tend to your own serious illness, or to care for family members who have serious health conditions. Employees who work for large companies and who have worked for that company for at least a year are eligible to take this unpaid leave. For more information on whether or not you are eligible to take this leave, you can download the National Partnership for Women & Families' Guide to FMLA at www.nationalpartnership.org or visit the Department of Labor at www.dol.gov/dol/allcfr/ESA/Title_29/Part_825/toc.htm.

• Check with your state's department of labor to see what is available to you: Some states have standards for family and medical leave that are more generous than the federal law. In many states, employees who work for small- or medium-size companies are eligible to take 12 weeks of unpaid leave. In other states, workers may take more time off or may take leave for reasons other than those specified by the FMLA.

• Find out whether you are eligible for Temporary Disability Insurance (TDI). TDI programs provide partial wage replacement to employees who are temporarily disabled for non-work-related reasons, including pregnancy disability. The states that require employers to provide TDI are California, Rhode Island, New Jersey, New York, and Hawaii; Puerto Rico also requires TDI. Employers in other states sometimes voluntarily offer TDI as an employee benefit. California has recently passed an extention to their TDI program. Beginning in July 2004, eligible California workers can receive 55% to 60% of their wages for up to 6 weeks while they care for a newborn or adopted baby. For more information about this law, please visit www.edd.ca.gov/difla.htm.

• If possible, take advantage of at-home infant-care programs: Low-income parents living in Minnesota or Montana may be able to take advantage of these programs, which allow eligible parents to receive subsidies while they care for their own children—instead of paying to put them in day care. For example, in Minnesota, new parents can contact the Minnesota Department of Children, Families and Learning at 651-852-8200 or visit www.educ.state.mn.us, and in Montana, new parents can contact the Montana Department of Public Health and Human Services at 406-444-5900 or visit www.dphhs.state.mt.us.

value of employer-sponsored benefits is estimated by some to be 20% to 25% of base salary, so benefits—in whatever form—can be a huge help. You may even want to go so far as to write "as many as possible" under the heading "Benefit Needs" on your bookmark. But bear in mind, too, that if you are a low-income mother, many big-ticket employer-sponsored benefits (like child care and health care) may be unaffordable or may be set up in a way that is cost prohibitive. So you'll need to do your research here and look to outside resources for additional support, some of which I've listed in boxes.

Exercise

Get out that bookmark again. If you have not done so already, write down what remaining benefits you need, if any. Under the Benefits heading, you should be listing the big-ticket items that are common and that you feel you need. They should be ones that you can realistically hope to get if not at a small employer than at a large one. When you get to the stage of approaching an employer, you'll probably want to be thinking about the totality of benefits provided by that employer, particularly if money is tight. Remember, benefits equal a good portion of base salary. You also should be thinking about how a change in employment might change your child-care costs, if at all, and whether you could afford that under your current income needs. If not, you should add that cost to the figure you've listed under "Income Needs."

Real Mother Recap

Here's the quick summary: You should finish this section with a clear idea of your needs. If you don't need benefits, you are not limited in terms of the arrangements you can seek. If you do need benefits, however, some forms of part-time work and self-employment might not work for you. Once more, as you think about your overall needs, realize what's family-friendly to you might not be for someone else. Needs are relative, and hence so is the term *family-friendly work*.

NOTES

Introduction

1. From information provided by more than 15,000 respondents, researchers found that, in average households, women control over 75% of the finances and are responsible for 80% of purchasing decisions. Proctor & Gamble, Harris Interactive, and Woman.com Network, *The Online Woman: How to Tap into Her Buying Powers* (November 1999).

2. Bureau of Census for the Bureau of Labor Statistics, *Current Population Survey, 2001* (Washington, DC: U.S. Department of Labor, 2003). Available at: www.dol.gove/wb/faz38.htm; accessed on March 28, 2003.

3. The labor force participation rate for mothers with children under 18 was 72.1% in 2001. *Employment Characteristics of Families Summary*, March 2002. Bureau of Census for the Bureau of Labor Statistics,

Current Population Survey, 2001 (Washington, DC: U.S. Department of Labor, 2002).

4. According to the U.S. Census Bureau, the labor force participation of mothers with infant children was 59% in 1998 and 55% in 2000. Amara Bachu and Martin O'Connell, *Fertility of American Women: June 2000* [Current Population Reports P20-543RV] (Washington, DC: Census Bureau, 2001).

5. In a study of 2,000 managers from four companies, Catalyst noted that 36% of women managers will have worked part-time at some point in their careers. Catalyst, *A New Approach to Flexibility: Managing the Work/Time Equation* (underwritten by the Alfred P. Sloan Foundation, 1997). Available at: www.catalystwomen.org/press_room/press_releases/new_approach_flexibility.htm; accessed on March 29, 2003.

6. According to statistics derived from the U.S. Bureau of the Census. Cited in Center for Women's Business Research, *Women-Owned Businesses in the United States, 2002: A Fact Sheet* (underwritten by Wells Fargo Bank, 2001). Available at: www.nfwbo.org/USStateFacts/US.pdf; accessed on: March 14, 2003.

7. Based on median employee tenure of 3.9 years for men and 3.4 years for women. *Employee Tenure Summary,* September 2002. Bureau of Census for the Bureau of Labor Statistics, *Current Population Survey, 2002* (Washington, DC: U.S. Department of Labor, 2002). Available at: www.bls.gov/news.release/tenure.nr0.htm; accessed on: March 29, 2003.

Chapter 1

1. Arlie Russell Hochschild, *The Time Bind: When Work Becomes Home and Home Becomes Work* (New York: Metropolitan Books, 1997).

2. Ellen Galinsky, *Ask the Children: The Breakthrough Study That Reveals How to Succeed at Work and Parenting* (San Francisco: HarperSanFrancisco, 2000).

3. Bureau of Census for the Bureau of Labor Statistics, *Highlights of*

Women's Earnings in 1998 [Report 928] (Washington, DC: U.S. Department of Labor, April 1999). Jane Waldfogel found that married women earn only 57% of what men earn; see her "Understanding the Family Gap in Pay for Women and Children," *Journal of Economic Perspectives* 12, no. 1 (winter, 1998): 37–156. See difference of wages of mothers versus nonmothers in Paula England and Michelle J. Budig, "The Effects of Motherhood on Wages in Recent Cohorts: Findings from the National Longitudinal Survey of Youth": [unpublished manuscript] (University of Arizona, Tucson, Department of Sociology, 1998).

4. Catalyst, *Entrepreneurial Ideas Motivate Women to Start Businesses,* (New York: February 24, 1998). Media release for study entitled *Paths to Entrepreneurship: New Directions for Women in Business.* (Underwritten by Catalyst, The National Foundation of Women Business Owners, and the Committee of 200). Available at: www.catalystwomen.org/press_room/press_releases/entrepreneurs.htm; accessed on March 30, 2003.

Chapter 3

1. Anne Wilson Schaef, "June 2," in *Meditations for Women Who Do Too Much* (San Francisco: HarperSanFrancisco, 1990).

Chapter 4

1. Bureau of Census for the Bureau of Labor Statistics, *Highlights of Women's Earnings in 2001* [Report 960] (Washington, DC: U.S. Department of Labor, May 2002).

2. National Center for Health Statistics, *Deaths: Final Data for 1999.* National Vital Statistics Report Volume 49, No. 8. (Washington, DC: National Center for Health Statistics, 2001)

3. Census 2000 data show 2.1 million divorced women age 55 to 64 compared to 1.5 million widowed women of the same age (Table PCT7). The comparable figures from 1990 are 1.2 million and 1.8 million, respectively. (The Current Population Survey shows the change occurring in the mid to late 1990s, see reports for 1995 to 1997). Bureau of

Census for the Bureau of Labor Statistics, *Census 2000,* Table PCT7 (Washington, DC: U.S Department of Labor, 2003). Bureau of Census for the Bureau of Labor Statistics, *Census 1990* (Washington, DC: U.S. Department of Labor, 1992). Confirmed by Fertility and Family Statistics Branch, Population Division, Bureau of the Census, April 1, 2003.

4. Naomi Drew, *Peaceful Parents, Peaceful Kids: Practical Ways to Create a Calm and Happy Home* (New York: Kensington Books, 2000).

Chapter 5

1. According to a survey of 945 major U.S. employers conducted by Hewitt Associates, some form of health, life, retirement—including 401(k)s—and dental insurance plans were among the most commonly offered benefits. Hewitt Associates, "Salaried Employee Benefits Provided by Major U.S. Employers 2001–2002." (Lincolnshire, Illinois: Hewitt Associates, LLC 2001). They were also among the most common in a survey of 551 human resource professionals in the United States by the Society for Human Resource Management (SHRM). SHRM Survey Program, 2002 Benefits Survey (Alexandria, VA: SHRM, 2002).

STEP TWO

Identify Your Strengths

6

Learn Your Points of Leverage

Women who can run children already have all the business skills. . . . If you can do all that, doing a business pales in comparison.

—AMILYA

AMILYA

Amilya Antonetti, CEO of the California-based company Soapworks, is a woman with a mission. Seven years ago her infant son, David, was very ill. After much research, she found her son was highly allergic to common ingredients in many cleaning products—part of a condition she says is now called multiple chemical syndrome. She also saw that many other children were suffering from some of the same ailments as her son's. So she put an ad in the local bargain sheet inviting parents to join her at a hotel to discuss the need for better products in their homes. Hundreds of women showed up. Then she started making soap from a recipe that her grandmother had. She passed the soap among friends and among some of those women who responded to her ad. They liked it. They wanted more. Soap making moved from her kitchen to her garage; and one year later, after she had maxed out about

50 credit cards and sold the house and the car, Soapworks was on its way of taking on the big boys of the multi-million-dollar U.S. laundry-detergent market. Amilya's mission to supply hypoallergenic cleansing products to mothers was paying off.

So, how did she do it, really? Amilya attributes many factors to her success, but perhaps first among them is this: "I took my parenting skills and applied it to business." In fact, she believes so adamantly in the skills that parenting can bring that among the first questions she asks potential hires is whether they have kids and given that, how they manage their days. "Women who can run children already have all the business skills. . . . Women so naturally multitask," she says, pointing to the old adage that when you want something done, ask the busiest person you know. In fact, so convinced is she that parents—and particularly mothers—bring value to her business that about 90% of her employees are female; about 70% are parents, and her advisory board is made up exclusively of mothers. "They bring what is really going on in the world today." To retain those employees, she offers benefits rare in Corporate America. In addition to a very accommodating flex policy— "There will be no soccer game you will miss"—and the freedom to bring children to work, employees get dirty clothes laundered at work and groceries delivered as well. She's even considering opening a school at work to help parents cope.

To date, Amilya's efforts have worked. She never once has had to ask an employee to stay late. They do what they know they must. Meanwhile, her company continues to grow both in reach and in size with products available in over 2,500 retail outlets nationwide and revenues doubling every year. And as her company expands, her profile grows through her brand and through the increased attention she is generating in the media across the United States.

Yet despite her success, Amilya still seems—perhaps above all else—a mom. She's a woman struggling to do it all but aware that all will never be done. And she's okay with that. For while some may call her idealistic in the way she believes a company can be run, she's realistic about what she can expect of herself. She's not perfect and she wants mothers to know that first and foremost. "I'm okay with all my little imperfections. Show me your fat and I'll show you mine," she jokes. "Cellulite is a sign of life."

Okay, so now you have an idea of your needs, or at least I hope you do. If you don't, send the kids back to their father, grandfather, or unsuspecting uncle, and read that section again. But assuming that Step One has triggered some sort of thought process in that overdriven brain of yours, it's time to move on to Step Two: Identify Your Strengths.

Your primary strengths when it comes to getting family-friendly work are your skills, your knowledge, and your network. These are what give you value in the workplace and give you leverage in getting an arrangement that works. These are what this section is about. "You need to know your value and sell it," says Bruce Tulgan, a management consultant and author who has spent a lot of time looking at how today's employers and employees can benefit each other most. You need to "concentrate on your strengths," as one CEO said to Helen, a single mother of two in Utah who works in advertising. To this day, she says, it is the most valuable message she ever got.

Sounds obvious, but as you look for your family-friendly job, it can be easy to lose sight of that fact. When I ran a career magazine, I often received e-mail from women saying that they wanted to work from home and did I have any ideas of jobs they could pursue?

My response to those women and to you is this: First think about why you want a particular arrangement. Think, as I suggested in Step One, about your children's needs, your personal needs, and your financial needs. What specifically do you want from your job? Then, think about your greatest strengths—namely, your skills, contacts, and knowledge base—something I'll ask you to do in the next few chapters of this book. Once you've done those two things, you can start considering how well a particular arrangement will work for you and whether you have a shot at getting that arrangement. You can use your network to research these facts. If, for example, you have decided you need to be accessible to your kids when they are small, based on your experience and the experiences of others you know, which skills and knowledge areas will give you enough leverage to secure such an arrangement? Which skills and knowledge areas will an employer or prospective employer value enough to be willing to set up a nontraditional arrangement?

In fact, again and again in my interviews, women tell me in no uncertain terms that their family-friendly arrangement works because they consistently perform, regardless of the type of position they hold. They have the skills, knowledge, and contacts to make it work. I don't invite those comments. They offer them unsolicited, ready to justify their arrangement in real terms to anyone who asks. Says one public relations executive from Little Rock, Arkansas, who works full-time from home and who has what she calls an unusual level of flexibility to manage family and work, "It depends on results, on what you produce." States another market researcher from St Paul, Minnesota: "Hours I put into work are not important, what matters is that the job is done well." Agrees another executive recruiter and mother to two school-age children in Massachusetts, "The bottom line is getting the job done. If you want that flexibility, you must make sure work doesn't suffer." "It's all about adding value," says another mother from Denver, Colorado, when explaining her repeated success in securing a series of family-friendly jobs.

Of course, the stronger and more relevant your network, skills, and knowledge base, the better off you'll be. Unfair? Perhaps. But consider it from an employer's perspective. A relevant set of skills, a knowledge base, and a network make you desirable. They give an employer the confidence that you'll get the job done, even given the terms you demand. Why do you think U.S. Census Bureau statistics show that first-time mothers in their 30s are far more likely to receive paid maternity benefits than younger mothers?[1] As I've said before, if your employer is going to give you added benefits—through telecommuting capabil-ity, paid maternity leave, part-time, or flexible work weeks—that em-ployer needs to know that you can deliver, despite what may be the perceived or actual costs of your family-friendly demands. The more successful you are in providing that assurance, the better off you'll be. Why do you think executive recruiters say it is far easier to get a part-time or flexible position once you're in a full-time job or through people for whom you've done work in the past? Why do you think Kylie, a mother to a toddler from Louisiana, was able to convince her employer to let her be the first in her company to go part-time? You guessed it, these employees showed they could get the job done.

Where There's Hope Yet

But even if you don't have the strongest or most relevant network, knowledge base, or skills set, you still may be able to get family-friendly work. If you have little education, you may have to go back to school to get further education. If your profession isn't family-friendly, you may have to retrain. If you've been out of the work-force for a long time, you may have to lower your job sights, volunteer in a relevant field, or get additional training through coursework. But depending on your needs, you may still be able to get the job you need. Why? Well, part of the reason is that although the workplace is still far from ideal, you may have more leverage now than U.S. women ever have had before. Women now make up almost half of the nation's labor pool, and a growing proportion of them are more qualified, more senior, and more committed to the workforce than ever before. Because of that, more and more com-panies are striving to accommodate the mothers and fathers they employ. They are beginning to acknowledge the demands parents face. Most of America's major U.S. employers, for example, now of-fer some form of child-care assistance and almost three quarters offer flexible scheduling arrangements.[2] Arrangements like these not only are necessary but help attract the talent employers need.

In addition, some companies are realizing that women are a lifeline into one of the most coveted segments of the American economy—the consumer. Remember, women in America today control more than 80% of household and personal spending decisions and make 75% of their family's financial choices. Because of figures like these, visionaries like best-selling author Tom Peters maintains that "women are big opportunity No. 1" and recommends that Corporate America pay heed fast by employing women in top roles and getting more in touch with their needs. Peters notes that the jock strap was invented in 1874 but the sports bra had to wait until 1977 to be invented, with some 42 million sold in 1996, according to *Women's Sports & Fitness*.[3] (Men didn't see that opportunity until some 100 years later because they were too busy looking after their own equipment, I say.) Peters's view is echoed by consultants like Faith Popcorn who spends her time identifying business trends. Among her views? The importance of targeting women in successfully marketing a brand.[4]

The point is that visionaries like these are not alone. Some companies also are bending their collective ears to women's voices because they think their businesses can benefit from paying a little more attention to what a women perceives. Legions of forward-thinking companies are making strident efforts to incorporate more women into all levels of their organizations from Avon—led by mother-of-two CEO Andrea Jung—to countless members of the car industry who are at last recognizing that women figure significantly into car-buying decisions. Or look at the lending company Fannie Mae, which reports that close to half of its management employees and over half of its employees are now women, while almost a quarter of its management and more than 40% of its employees are minorities.[5] Why have they striven so hard to get those figures so high? One reason is that composition gives them a more accurate perspective on the housing market, they say.

In fact, one need only look at the rate at which women are now starting businesses—at twice the rate of men—to see that women can identify niches that big companies have missed. Yes, that germ of an idea that won't go away may be worth something. Take, for example, a woman I interviewed named Heidi. She was a serious scientist—Yale educated and working as a biologist on a project that won the Nobel Prize in chemistry. "My thesis teacher said we should eat, breathe, walk, talk biology, and he was serious," she says of that world. "There are," she explains, "very few female, high-level professors and the few there don't have kids because it is very demanding and it takes all of your time." Unwilling to give that kind of time to her work while also being a parent, Heidi took a leave of absence. While on that leave of absence, her two-year-old daughter started to ask typical questions of that age (don't feel badly, mine never did to this extent, and they're still doing okay): Why is the sky blue? Why do leaves change colors? When Heidi tried to find a book to answer these questions in a way that a small child would understand, she found nothing. So she started her own company, Little Scientists, with a mission to teach science to children from preschool through third grade.

Now, Little Scientists is a franchise business with close to 30 operations worldwide, some of them as far abroad as Japan, and each year it continues to grow. Yes, Heidi does have a Ph.D. from Yale, but she started her business based primarily on her experience with her two-year-old daughter and her unwavering interest in science.

Amilya did the same based on her experience with her newborn son. They identified their businesses *because* they are moms, not despite it. And who, do you think, makes up a significant percentage of these companies' employee base? You guessed it—moms.

"Here's an idea for you," says Lilly, a former and still sometime dressmaker and mother of two, as she reaches into her black handbag for a credit card. "A little light that turns on when you open your purse." "Great idea," responds her friend. "Women tend to have black purses, black handbags. That works." And on they chat.

Another business idea that some handbag maker missed because he didn't reach into his little black handbag at night.

Believe in Yourself

Of course, that awareness won't get you a family-friendly job. Nor will it make you successful once you're employed. Most employers won't hire you because you carry some unique knowledge as a woman or because they need women to fill jobs. But a growing number of women in the workplace who have the desired skills, knowledge, and/or networks are compelling employers to take note. They (and some family-minded men) are succeeding in creating job arrangements that better accommodate their needs. A growing number of women in their own businesses are doing the same.

The point is that you can take advantage of this trend. You can identify your needs and strengths and, if necessary, build on those strengths where you must. Then, you can seek out your family-friendly arrangement by learning to successfully leverage your strengths.

Real Mother Recap

So you've finished the easy chapter for Step Two—the chapter without the work. I hope you've learned something nonetheless. You've learned that skills, network, and knowledge are key to getting family-friendly work. You may have known that already, but mothers are programmed to remind, regardless of whether the audience claims to need it or not.

7

Pinpoint Your Skills and Knowledge Areas

Once I knew what I liked about law and what my skills were, I set out to see what other types of jobs would use those skills best, and importantly, what I would enjoy doing.

—LONNIE

LONNIE

I spent a solid six months searching myself and researching my options. I followed a book called What Can You Do with a Law Degree?—*the* What Color Is Your Parachute? *for lawyers. I took quiz after quiz, assessment after assessment, to ascertain what it was about the law that I liked, what it was that I disliked, and to pinpoint my strengths and weaknesses exactly. I went so far in this as to even explore what kind of environment I work best in, whether I like people around, and what my office space should look like.*

I cannot begin to tell you how much I learned about myself. I learned that what I enjoyed about the law was the writing, the process of quiet-but-persistent persuasion, the thoughtful aspects of practicing law—not the dramatic parts, like being in front of the jury and acting as mediator between two angry parties. What I disliked vehemently was being in the middle of discourse, of battle, of disagreement. I had to even admit that I didn't love having to relate to people I just couldn't relate to.

I also learned that my biggest obstacle to moving on in another field would be giving up the status of being an attorney (and the money, but mostly the status). I struggled with that. I also was afraid that a major career change would disappoint my husband and family. Once I convinced my husband that I was sure of what I was doing (which came only after I had to convince myself), he was completely supportive, even in the face of my law school student loan payments that were still owed. He wanted me to be happy, and he believed in my ability to earn a certain income. And neither of us has ever looked back.

Once I knew what I liked about law, and what my skills were, I set out to see what other types of jobs would use those skills best, and importantly, what I would enjoy doing. One of the careers I researched was grant writing. I came to see that writing strong, competitive grants takes skill in not only writing but also in analysis and logic, all of which my background in the law well equipped me for. I had a strong hunch the solitary nature of this work, and the positive impact it could make without all the discourse, would be well suited to me. So I set out to convince someone take a chance on me, since I had no experience.

I started scouring the want ads and sent out résumé after résumé with little positive response. I then moved on to networking. Funny story—I saw a PR piece in my local paper about a former utilities lawyer who was now the director of communications at the local community college. So I called her up to see if we could meet for coffee and chat about how she made the leap from lawyer to PR person. She agreed, and we sat down and chatted for about an hour. I sent her a follow-up thank-you note and let it go. Well, a few months later I was lucky enough to get an interview with a grants consulting firm and I convinced them to take a chance on me. I also took a $15,000 pay cut. Within a year, I was up to the *same amount I had made practicing law. Three years ago, a friend in the company referred me to someone at a college who was looking for a director to write grants, and it turned out to be the same local community college where I met the other lawyer-turned-administrator. After I met with my [potential] supervisor, she spoke to the other former lawyer, who had nice things to say about me, and now we are all here. We even have another former female lawyer at the college in a different position. The law is the best-kept secret for finding well-rounded women with great skills who are dying to move into something else.*

So let's begin identifying your skills and knowledge areas. As I mentioned, these are important leverage points for getting the job you need. What I didn't mention is that the job that you need may not be the one you thought.

The truth is that while getting a job can be difficult, getting a family-friendly job can be more difficult. Thinking laterally about your skills and your knowledge may provide you with job options you might otherwise overlook. Take Lonnie, the mother of two who was featured at the start of this chapter. She believed strongly that law could not meet her needs, so she spent a solid six months better understanding those needs and her passions, identifying her skills, and researching her options. One of the careers to which her skills led her was grant writing, the family-friendly job that she now holds.

As you consider the job that's right for you, you also have to recognize that it may not make use of your full repertoire of skills or knowledge. "You need to look at your skill set as if it were in a brief-case," says Kathleen Shelby, a working mother and founder of the New Jersey–based interim staffing company called FlexTime Solutions, Inc. You may pull out some skills for one job and different ones for another. That's okay. Remember: By committing yourself to your kids *and* your work, you are straddling two worlds. The more weight you put in your kids' world, the less weight you put in your work. "When you work full-time you look at yourself as that job," says Shelby when explaining the difficulty some women have in accepting what may be diminished responsibility in their family-friendly work, particularly if it's part-time. "When you go part-time, you make a trade-off. A lot of people see that as a deficit. We talk to people who say, I can do a lot more than that. What we say is that what you may have to sacrifice is not using all your skill set."

Of course, not every family-friendly job will force you to draw on a more limited selection of skills or knowledge. Some full-time and even some part-time women with family-friendly work believe they have made little compromise in the satisfaction they derive from their work or in the range of skills they employ. But many do make that compromise, a compromise that by no means undermines the importance of their strengths. Remember Claire who was introduced at the start of this book? By the time I finished writing the manuscript, she was divorced and working within a large publishing house, filling the roles of a succession of employees who were taking maternity leave. The strength of her skills and her knowledge not only allowed her to have the opportunity to cover those positions but also allowed her to work a shortened week. Did her skills overqualify her? Perhaps. But that overqualification helped secure those family-friendly jobs.

Last, as you think about your skills and knowledge, don't underestimate the skills or knowledge areas you've acquired through unpaid experiences. Those experiences may include school, hobbies, interests, volunteering, or simply being a mom. When Amilya communicated the need for products like hers to industry veterans, they told her she had to be joking. Buyers for grocery stores told her that none of their customers would be interested in her hypoallergenic cleansing products. What did she know? She had no experience in the business. But she did have experience with her own child. The knowledge she gained from that experience, combined with her innate skills, was enough to successfully build her business and prove them wrong.

While being a mother won't get you a job, it does draw on skills that are relevant in today's workplace. Congresswoman Nancy Pelosi, a now 62-year-old mother to five children who didn't return to paid employment until her youngest child was a high school senior, put it this way to *Working Mother:*

> I can tell you that being a mom was great training for the job that I have now. With five kids there are 20 ways to have an argument. So I acquired certain diplomatic skills, which, I find, are coming in quite handy. There's the ability to head off confrontation, the tactics of confrontation and diversion, and just the ability to appreciate the mood that someone might be in at any given time.[1]

Pelosi became the Minority leader in the U.S. House of Representatives.

As I said, you won't be able to convince an employer to create a family-friendly position simply because you can get the kids dressed, make breakfast, prepare lunch, put away the dishes, mediate an argument, avert a meltdown, and get to the bus in the time it takes some people to read the paper, pass pleasantries, and go through the morning's correspondences. Nor will they hire you because you, unlike some men, can do two tasks at once. Most employers probably won't hire you because of these skills (though Amilya might). Most also won't hire you on the knowledge you've gained from raising kids or on knowledge you've gained from interests and unpaid work alone. But you can use those experiences to help identify your strongest skills and fields of knowledge and to determine how they might lend themselves to other types of work. You might even be able to use some of them to help demonstrate your interest in a job and build related contacts, depending on the job you want. If you haven't worked for a long time and you're interested in teaching, for example, you may be able to volunteer as an assistant in your child's school. Supplement that with the necessary qualifications and you may be able to make a reasonably compelling case to be hired at that school should a position open up. If you haven't worked for a long time and you're interested in working in medicine, you could get your first aid and CPR qualifications and volunteer for your town's EMT. If you haven't worked for a long time and you're interested in philanthropic work, you might be able to get a volunteer position at a nonprofit and then ultimately segue that into a job that's paid. But whatever you do, don't sell those experiences short to yourself or to anyone else.

Let's Begin

So where do you start? As I mentioned in the last chapter, your skills are among your most important strengths when determining where your leverage lies in getting family-friendly work. Experts often classify skills into three groups: functional/transferable, job content (or work content), and self-management. Sounds unnecessarily complex, I know. Bear with me, and you'll begin to see why these categories make sense.

Functional Skills

Let's start with functional or transferable skills. Of all three categories, this one is the one that career counselors like to stress. Functional or transferable skills are natural abilities that you have that can transfer from one job to another. They are skills—such as analyzing, selling, or organizing—that you probably won't have acquired through work, though you may have strengthened them there. In fact, these skills often show up early in life. For example, perhaps you've always been good at selling. You were the top seller of magazine subscriptions for your school when you were a child, and as a mother, you sold the greatest number of cookbooks for school fund-raising efforts. Perhaps there are other skills you possess that continued to demonstrate themselves in your role as mother. You are good at heading off confrontation. You're extremely sensitive to people's moods. You didn't need a paid job to get those skills. But to do well in some jobs, you need them.

The reason that many career coaches stress these skills is that clients often seek a coach because they are dissatisfied in their work. By identifying a client's transferable skills, that coach will be able to help the client come up with a range of jobs to which her skills apply. Then the client will need to convince an employer of just how good those transferable skills are. As a mother who wants a job on terms that work for her, you'll need to do the same. If you're currently employed and seeking simply to alter the arrangement under which you currently work, these skills will not be as relevant, because you already will have proven them in your work. But if you're seeking to change your position within your company or go to work for someone else, you will benefit from being able to identify these skills.

Pinpointing Your Transferable Skills

Where do you start? To help you identify your strongest transferable skills, I suggest looking at this list put together by Richard Knowdell, a California-based career coach/trainer. It is based on the 51 skills cards in his "Motivated Skills Card Sort" kit. Knowdell has kindly agreed to let me reproduce the skills on his cards. Take a moment to do the following:

- Read the list once, crossing out your weakest skills and those that you positively don't enjoy. If you have a strong skill that

MOTIVATED SKILLS CARD SORT*

COMPUTER LITERATE
Develop, organize, and complete tasks and projects using software programs such as Microsoft *Word*, *Excel*, and *PowerPoint*.

PLAN AND ORGANIZE
Define goals and objectives; schedule and develop projects and programs.

OBSERVE
Study, scrutinize, and examine data, people, or things scientifically.

TEACH AND TRAIN
Inform, explain, give instruction to students, employees or customers.

WORK WITH NUMBERS
Easily calculate, compute, organize, understand, and solve numerical and quantitative problems.

MAKE ARANGEMENTS
Coordinate events; handle logistics.

ENTERTAIN AND PERFORM
Amuse, sing, dance, create art, or play music for an audience; give demonstrations.

READ FOR INFORMATION
Research written resources efficiently and exhaustively.

MONITOR
Keep track of the movement of data, people, or things.

NEGOTIATE
Bargain for rights or advantages.

DEAL WITH AMBIGUITY
Be comfortable and effective with issues that lack clarity, structure, or certainty.

COUNSEL
Facilitate insight and personal growth; guide, advise, or coach students, employees, or clients.

USE MECHANICAL ABILITIES
Assemble, tune, repair, or operate engines or other machinery.

ANALYZE
Break down and figure out problems logically.

EXPEDITE
Speed up production or services; trouble-shoot problems; streamline procedures.

PORTRAY IMAGES
Sketch, draw, illustrate, paint, photograph.

SUPERVISE
Oversee; direct the work of others.

TEST
Measure proficiency, quality, or validity; check and double-check.

WRITE
Compose reports, letters, articles, ads, stories, or educational materials.

MENTOR
Educate, guide, coach, or counsel a less-accomplished or junior colleague.

STRATEGIZE
Effectively plan and develop long-range strategies that successfully accomplish objectives.

SYNTHESIZE
Integrate ideas and information, combine diverse elements into a coherent whole.

RESEARCH ONLINE
Able to use search engines and the World Wide Web to gather and organize information and data.

PROOFREAD AND EDIT
Check writings for proper usage and stylistic flair; make improvements.

MANAGE TIME
Ability to prioritize, structure, and schedule tasks to maximize effort and meet deadlines.

MEDIATE
Manage conflict, reconcile differences.

CUSTOMER SERVICE
Effectively solve problems and challenges that satisfy customers.

MAINTAIN RECORDS
Keep accurate and up-to-date records; log, itemize, collate, and tabulate data.

ADAPT TO CHANGE
Easily and quickly respond to changing assignments, work settings, and priorities.

CLASSIFY
Group, categorize and systematize data, people, or things.

INTERVIEW FOR INFORMATION
Draw out subjects through incisive questioning.

CONCEPTUALIZE
Conceive and internally develop concepts and ideas.

BUDGET
Economize, save, and stretch money, and other sources.

SELL
Promote a person, company, goods, or services; convince of merits; raise money.

INITIATE CHANGE
Exert influence on changing the status quo; exercise leadership in bringing about new directions.

PERCEIVE INTUITIVELY
Sense; show insight and foresight.

MOTIVATE
Recruit involvement; mobilize energy; stimulate peak performance.

ACT AS LIAISON
Represent or serve as a link between individuals or groups.

DEAL WITH FEELINGS
Draw out, listen, accept, empathize, express sensitivity, defuse anger, calm, inject humor, appreciate.

IMPLEMENT
Provide detailed follow-through of policies and plans.

TEAM WORK
Easily and effectively work with others to obtain results.

IMPROVISE
Effectively think, speak, and act without preparation.

GENERATE IDEAS
Reflect on, conceive of, dream up, brainstorm ideas.

ESTIMATE
Appraise value or cost.

VISUALIZE
Imagine possibilities; see in mind's eye.

EVALUATE
Assess, review, and critique feasibility or quality.

MULTITASK
Effectively manage a variety of tasks and projects simultaneously.

INNOVATE AND INVENT
Create unique ideas or combine existing ideas to obtain a new or unique result.

DESIGN
Structure new or innovative practices, programs, products, or environments.

DELEGATE
Achieve effective results by assigning tasks to others.

MAKE DECISIONS
Make major, complex, or frequent decisions.

you dislike, still cross it out. It is what is known as a "burnout" skill; you'll tire of using that skill fast. Yes, in your family-friendly work, you may be compelled to use one of these skills. But be aware that if you use burnout skills too often, you will begin to feel dissatisfied.

• Read the list again, this time circling remaining skills at which you are proficient or very proficient. Then, under the heading "Transferable Skills" on your bookmark, list those you've circled. You may have some 5 to 15. These will be the skills you may end up pursuing in your family-friendly work.

• On a separate sheet of paper, record each transferable skill. Beneath each one, list ways you've effectively used that skill in past work or personal experiences. For example, one of my skills is "Interview for Information." Beneath that skill, I will list my work interviewing hundreds of women for this book and my specific experiences as a print and radio journalist. I might even include a note to myself that I often interview people in social situations and on the phone when I'm trying to garner information on behalf of my children, and think of specific instances for which I've done exactly that. I will also note that I enjoy using that skill, and I feel it comes naturally to me. All of those experiences—particularly my work-related ones—may prove helpful to me as a point of reference when I'm asked in my search for family-friendly work why I am qualified to do a particular job on the terms I seek.

• Lastly, among those skills you have not circled or crossed out, you may find skills you really enjoy but which you have not developed. Write those skills down on that same additional sheet of paper under the term "To Be Developed." These may be skills that you'd like to develop in the future. Pursuing those skills—through course work, unpaid work, supplemental projects, or other avenues—may serve as a way for you to fulfill some of those personal and professional needs that you may have had to compromise for family-friendly work.

Understanding Your Self-Management

The second category is self-management skills. As the term suggests, these pertain to the way you best manage yourself when working. They are, in effect, personality traits. To determine them, you need to look at yourself and figure out, given your personality, under what context you work best. Do you work best independently or in a team, intuitively or methodically, under pressure or at your own pace? These will not directly help you get a job, but knowing which skills you have in this area can be useful in identifying what kind of job, company culture, and job arrangement best suits you. Again, to identify these, you need to look at how you work in paid and unpaid situations. After you inventory these skills (see the next page), record your answers to questions 1 and 2 on your bookmark under "Self-Management Skills." You will revisit questions 3 and 4 later in the book.

And Now Work-Content Skills and Knowledge Bases

Last come your work-content skills and your knowledge bases. Work-content skills, unlike the other two categories of skills, relate to a specific job or occupation. They are skills that you've acquired—usually through schooling, work-related experience, training, or simply your own hard work—that qualify you for a specific job. They don't have to stem from paid work, but often they do. Examples of specific work-content skills include taking vitals if you're a nurse, fixing cars if you're a mechanic, operating a switchboard if you're a receptionist,

Self-Management Skills Inventory*

To inventory your self-management skills, Richard Knowdell suggests describing yourself in terms of adverbs—"ly"—words. These, along with the values you identified in the preceding section, will be useful when assessing whether a corporate culture, position, and/or arrangement are right for you.

Inventory your self-management skills—the distinctive manner by which you conduct yourself, how you do things.

1. Describe yourself in terms of adverbs ("ly" words); for example, *independently, persistently, creatively.*

2. Star the items on your list that are especially dominant qualities.

3. What job roles would make good use of your self-management skills?

4. What job settings would most readily accommodate your self-management skills?

*Copyright 2002 Richard L. Knowdell. Reprinted with permission.

and writing articles if you're a print journalist. As you complete the exercise below, focus on identifying your strongest work-content skills. These will probably be related to jobs and experiences that are recent or that you feel you could easily refresh through a course or some attention at home. Also, remember that if you enjoy using those work-content skills, you'll be happier down the line. So pay special attention to work-content skills that you enjoy.

Note that this exercise includes knowledge areas as a work-content skill. You should feel that you have a thorough understanding of the knowledge areas you write down. Again, ideally, they should interest

Work-Content Skills Inventory*

Again, Richard Knowdell has kindly given me permission to use one of his exercises. Here's how this one works: Inventory your technical abilities and the specialized knowledges you have acquired through formal and informal means. Star items that you would like to focus on in your future career.

WORK-CONTENT SKILLS AND SPECIAL KNOWLEDGES DEVELOPED IN

· School:

· Work:

· Play:

*Copyright © 2002 by Richard L. Knowdell. Reprinted with permission.

you as well, as it is hard to sustain a job if you do not like the area to which it pertains. Realize, too, that you can still list a knowledge area if you enjoy it but need further qualification to bring it to a level at which it qualifies you for employment. If, for example, real estate is your passion and you know the sale price of every home in your neighborhood in the last year, you'll still need a license if you want to enter into sales. That doesn't mean, however, that you can't list that knowledge here. After you have completed the exercise, record your answers under "Work-Content Skills" on your bookmark.

Exercise

Now, I hope you've taken the time to consider your three areas of skills and your knowledge base. If your children pulled you away, go back when you have a moment and do these exercises before you

---

Skills Cue Card

Having trouble remembering which skill is which? One career coach I interviewed provides her clients these clues:

- **Transferable skills:** Think *action;* think *verb.* Example: writing.

- **Self-management skills:** Think *adverb/adjective;* think *how.* Example: independently.

- **Work-content skills:** Think *noun.* Example: real estate sales.

---

move ahead in the book. If you have completed them, be sure you recorded your answers on your bookmark. Realize, as you write those answers down, that if you intend either to alter your role within your current organization or to find a new family-friendly job altogether, these are the skills and knowledge areas from which you'll want to draw. They will be key in getting work on terms that are right for you. If you are reentering the job market after a long time away, you'll no doubt have had to think harder about your skills. You'll have had to consider volunteer work you've done and experiences you've had that quantify your skills. If you have little education or few work-related skills, you'll obviously have less leverage in getting the arrangement you need, particularly if you need the full amount of income that your skills command. But that doesn't mean you can't build your skills on the job, supplementing it through on-site training and further education outside work. In fact, your ideal family-friendly employer may be one who provides for just that.

Real Mother Recap

Skills are key in getting family-friendly work. For before you even think about securing an arrangement you want, you need to be sure you have the skills the job needs. The stronger those skills, the easier the task of convincing your employer that you can do the job. Strong and appropriate skills are, above all else, the leverage you need to get work on the terms you want. So take the time to identify yours.

If you need more help: Richard Knowdell's *Motivated Skills Card Sort Planning Kit* is a good resource. Call 408-441-9100 or visit his Web site to find out more (www.careertrainer.com).

8

Establish Your Network

I could not have juggled without my female support system.
—DONNA

DONNA

When public relations consultant Donna turned on the TV to see
a newscast of preschoolers being led away from a gun rampage in
California, she grew enraged. Something had to be done to stop
gun violence, she thought. Before long, she had come up with an
idea: a grass-roots-fueled mother's march on Washington, D.C.
She called her friend Debby, who is in marketing and whom she
had met through their kids' play group. "I can't believe you just
called," Debby said. She had seen the same report and immedi-
ately was on board with the cause. They then called Allison, who's
a writer; Robin, whose husband owns a women's clothing store;
and Amy, who's a graphic designer. Before long, these women
had 5,000 T-shirts—an ample launchpad for a campaign for
Donna. She also got a permit to march on the Mall in Washing-
ton, D.C. on Mother's Day.

The march that began with a televised newscast and a motivated mother ultimately drew some 750,000 men and women demanding tougher gun laws. And the momentum hasn't stopped there. In little over a year since that first march, the organization has grown to some 235 chapters across 46 states. To what does Donna attribute the success? "A grass-roots mother network," she says.

Donna, a mother of two children, is a testament to what a strong network can do, not only politically but personally as well. Before she met her friends, she had moved out of New York City, given birth to a child, and found life in the suburbs very tough. The friends who helped her put those building blocks in place were women she met through a play group. They were a lifeline to her then. "They took me out of the isolation," she says.

When she launched the Million Mom March, it was only natural that she turn to them again—both to get her concept off the ground and to help her cope. At that time, she was juggling organizing the march, a job-sharing arrangement in publicity, and the many demands that being a mother brings. "I could not have juggled without my female support system," she says of the time. These women "put their kids first and are absolutely giving, caring people," she says.

So what does a woman like Donna do next? After the job-sharing arrangement ended, she enjoyed a summer with her children; now Donna aims to return to the workforce, probably in public relations again. To find that work, she's spread the word among friends and among others in her network that she's looking for work. She knows her strategy can work. She used it to get the last job-sharing arrangement she had—securing a lead on what she estimates was her 20th phone call—and she'll use it again. "You can't be afraid to pick up the phone and verbalize what you want," she says. Thanks to the support of her network, she succeeds when doing just that.

So now I hope you have an idea of your skills—work content, transferable, and self-management—as well as your knowledge areas. Now it's time to look at that other key strength in getting family-friendly work: your network.

Network, you might say, I don't have much of that. Ahhh, but even the most reclusive among you do. No matter what your current state of employment—stay-at-home mother or part-time telecommuter or full-time worker—you have a network from which you can draw. You have fellow volunteers, friends, relatives, neighbors, classmates, and colleagues. You have people whom you have helped and who in return will help you. You have a support system that can help you in your professional and personal life. They don't have to be people to whom you are exceedingly close. They don't have to be high powered. Even that quiet, self-effacing neighbor may have knowledge from which you could benefit. Children's friends' parents, people you met on vacation, and people with whom you volunteer all might be able to help in different ways. In fact, many career advisers will point to the strength of weak ties in getting a network to work for you. Because people you know only vaguely are often the ones who can introduce you to people with whom you wouldn't otherwise connect.

How to Network

But before you even start to think about approaching that network, you have to consider networking rule number one: *To network, you have to give.* Or as Missy, a mother of two and a mentor at the investment bank at which she works, says: "In networking, you're only as good as what you give away." The point is that *networking* is not a dirty word. Nor should it be an intimidating one. It often is, as one career coach told me, simply the power of researching be-

Networking Sources

- Alumni networks
- Associations—community, professional, and special interest
- Business events
- Charity organizations
- Children's events
- Conferences
- Internet—professional mailing lists, chat rooms, bulletin boards
- Investment group

- Neighborhoods
- Play groups
- Relatives
- Religious groups
- School events
- Social groups
- Sporting events
- What else can you add?

lems, answer questions, or put ideas into practice. It's about giving and getting help, something that most mothers practice day in and day out.

But to do it most effectively, you need to start by focusing on the give. At work, that means showing that you have other people's interest at heart by producing quality work and supporting others in their quest to do the same. It means joining your company's mentoring group, if one exists. It means passing on helpful leads when you can. It means taking the time to provide helpful professional or personal advice when it's sought. It means reaching back when someone reaches out.

The same is true in the sphere outside work that includes your home, community, interest groups, schools, and professional networks. It means connecting with people and providing leads. It means offering insights or advice when sought. It means contributing expertise, advice, or sheer companionship at events, associations, clubs, and organizations when you can. It means taking the time at your daughter's game to find out a little about the person next to you on the sideline and what her interests are. It means contributing your skills, knowledge or sheer womanpower to help when you can and, as you do that, understanding the interests of those people whom you may one day help.

How a Network Can Help You Manage

Once you understand that, you can begin to draw on that network for help. These people whom you have helped, or may one day strive to help, can provide opportunities, advocacy, information, leads, and support. Once you're in a job, they can be a key support by "pounding the table for you," as one telecommuting, part-time, management consultant from Massachusetts pointed out, something she says telecommuting workers desperately need. They can be your mentor, "a key to success for women," says Jane, a former investment banker who attributes the success of women in her former industry to whether they have a mentor or not.

At home, they also can provide a lot. They can cover when you're juggling too much, as they did for Donna when she was working part-time and spearheading the 750,000-strong Million Mom March. They can share their experiences and insights in tackling issues that relate to your children, your community, and your work. They can be the back-of-the-head eyes that every mother has but no child can see.

How Your Network Can Help You Get Family-Friendly Work

But in addition to helping you manage work and home, a strong network also can help you get family-friendly work. They not only can provide information to help you determine what job, arrangement, or employer is right for you but can provide contacts that might lead to the job you ultimately want.

Remember Hayley? She had recently moved from a city to a coastal town in which she, her son, and her husband now lived. Having quit her job and, at the suggestion of her husband, taken the summer off, she became more involved with the community, volunteering to put together a slide show. Through that project, she met a person who started companies and then sold them off. He saw in her a skill set that he could use to grow his company. She also realized she knew his parents through church. He offered her a job and she took it, part-time.

Or follow the career path of Mary, a freelance journalist, who moved from one radio network to another news network on the heels of someone with whom she had worked. She had a baby, negotiated part-time, then later went to a start-up wire service, again part-time and again working directly with two people with whom she had already worked. She had another baby and after some time decided her children would be better served if she freelanced for the same company, for some of the same people, from home. "I think I will go back to working at an office again," she says of the time when her children are older and she feels she can. And when she does, no doubt she'll draw on those same contacts again.

Likewise, many of the jobs that Claire, the woman I mentioned at the start of the book, has held are somehow linked to one of three people whom she has known her entire career. Samantha, the mother to three I introduced in Chapter 1, has drawn on her network of colleagues she established when working full-time to secure every one of the telecommuting, part-time projects she's had. And Lonnie, that lawyer who's now a grant writer, found her current job through a colleague who alerted her to the position and secured it on the recommendation of another woman with whom she had an informational interview years back.

What these stories and others should tell you is that the power of a strong network can carry a person far when seeking out family-friendly work. That network may be built on friendship, good work, or even a gut feeling derived from an interview or a series of genuine exchanges that convince the contact that you are worth the effort that helping takes. But that network is key.

Depending on your current situation, you'll use that network to varying extents, all of which I'll discuss in greater detail in upcoming chapters of this book. If you have no idea what you want to do, for example, you can begin by using your network to research what areas interest you. If you know what you want to do, you can use that network to identify employers that may be right for you. If you are interviewing for a job, that work network can be a powerful tool in convincing your employer that you're right for the job, particularly if your job is in sales or client services. If you have a job, you can use that network to research the viability of potential arrangements given your and your company's needs. If you have an arrangement and a job, you can use that network to help manage and advocate for you.

Exercise

Take a moment to think about where you spend your life. To which organizations, associations, and groups do you belong? With which former colleagues or classmates do you keep up? Which neighbors do you know? With whom do you have even some small rapport at your church or synagogue? With whom do you have a relationship at your office or through your child's school? Under the "Network" heading on your bookmark, write all organizations and groups that contain people with whom you have some rapport. Next time you're in that environment, think about whom you have helped. Also think about

Networking Tips

GIVE TO GET

It may sound crass, but if you give, you'll get more back. If you pass on a lead to someone, that person will be more accommodating if you later ask for a lead back. That someone can be a mother at the playground or a colleague in the next cubicle. And giving is not limited to leads. Ask Donna what she gave to her friends in exchange for all the support she got, and she'll go blank. Don't underestimate the power of friendship as well.

DON'T UNDERESTIMATE YOUR NETWORK

When I tell people I'm writing a book, most people say, "Oh you must have had a powerful network to do that." I always smile because the people most instrumental in getting this project off the ground were a college friend, a mother to a friend of my then four-year-old daughter, and two people from my church. Yes, it did take months and months of work, but the network that enabled me lay right at my back door. People who can help you and whom you can help are all around. Don't underestimate their strengths.

DRAW ON YOUR CONNECTIONS

Start with people you know when trying to find people who can help you. It's advantageous if they have some interest in what you seek. If, for example, you're trying to find out about part-time work, try to find someone you know who's worked part-time. Don't end your conversation without getting a suggestion of someone else to whom you might speak. If your contact says it's okay, be sure to mention your mutual contact when you call.

RESEARCH

Before you call someone, know something about the person or organization you are calling. You want them to connect with you and nothing does that better than letting that person know you've put in the time to get the most out of what she has to say. "I prepared for every phone call. I read everything," says

Jane of the calls she made when starting her business. "I knew what questions I had to answer. They were impressed with my knowledge." Don't, by the way, forget the assistant's name when you call again. You want to build trust.

LET THEM KNOW WHAT YOU NEED

When you do need help from your network, be specific about what you seek. It might be guidance, advice, insights, or support. Don't be afraid to ask. Donna talked to some 20 people when she was looking for public relations work before she got her last job. She simply called them up and asked if they knew of any work that might fit her skills.

RESPECT

Don't take the information, advice, or time a contact gives for granted. Set a limit to how much time you'll take. Ask, if appropriate, to take notes. Write a thank-you letter for their time and advice, particularly if they gave time to help you out.

BUILD

If someone has helped you, don't let the end of the discussion be the end of your relationship. Record her contact information and anything noteworthy that you gleaned. Keep your mind open to how you can give back down the line—whether by passing on a lead or a magazine article or by helping in some other way.

Real Mother Recap

You now should have added your network onto your list of strengths. Why? Because a network is vital in securing and managing family-friendly work. Those within your network can advocate for you at home and at work. They can provide information, support, and advice. They can represent you when you're not around. Without them, without someone who gives you some kind of support, creating a life in which you can successfully work and parent will be difficult at best. Just make sure that in seeking help from those within your network that you also are prepared to give back.

If you need more help: try Harvey Mackay's book *Dig Your Well Before You're Thirsty: The Only Networking Book You'll Ever Need.*[1] If you're thinking of joining a large professional organization for women, one worth considering is the National Association of Female Executives (**www. nafe.com**).

where you could pass on a lead or provide advice where formerly perhaps you have not. Think about ways in which you can help those people. Help them, and one day they might do the same for you.

NOTES

Chapter 6

1. Kristin Smith, Barbara Downs, and Martin O'Connell, *Maternity Leave and Employment Patterns: 1961–1995* [Current Population Reports P70–79] (Washington, DC, U.S. Census Bureau, 2001).

2. Hewitt Associates, *Salaried Employee Benefits Provided by Major U.S. Employers 2001–2002* (Lincolnshire, IL: Hewitt Associates, 2001).

3. Tom Peters, *Circle of Innovation: You Can't Shrink Your Way to Greatness* (New York: Knopf, 1977). The information about the jock strap is on p. 401

4. That's a big message in Faith Popcorn and Lys Marigold, *EVEolution: The Eight Truths of Marketing to Women* (New York: Hyperion, 2000).

5. Fannie Mae, Diversity Fact Sheet. Fannie Mae Press Office. Washington, DC. April 30, 2002.

Chapter 7

1. Carolyn Hoyt, "Bulletin: A Friend in the House." *Working Mother,* May 2002, p. 22.

Chapter 8

1. Harvey Mackay, *Dig Your Well Before You're Thirsty: The Only Networking Book You'll Ever Need* (New York: Currency/Doubleday, 1997).

Understand the Work Arrangements

9

The Third Way

Over the last decade, I have seen such an increase in demand for flexible work options as well as an increased awareness and openness to it.

—RITA

RITA

"You evolve." That is how Rita, a human resources (HR) executive recruiter begins when explaining how she handles work and parenting demands. She is not all sage and wisdom, certain of every step she has taken, every decision she's made. *"I am my own worst enemy,"* she says. With her children now adolescents, she still sometimes asks herself. *"Did I do enough with [my children]? Was I on the floor enough?"* But then she looks back at how she has managed to divide work and parenting and stops herself. *"I was able to have the best of both worlds,"* she says.

Like many women, Rita put in her time at the start of her career. After the birth of her first child, she moved from working full-time in HR to work as an executive recruiter for another firm that specialized in her field. In a sales-driven role and being new to the firm, she worked hard that first year, sometimes 60-

hour weeks. Success was judged on performance above all else. But a year into her work, she realized something had to change. With two young children now, working and parenting had become too much. "I was ready to quit," she says.

Ready to give her notice, she approached her boss. He preempted her by suggesting she go part-time instead. "Because I had a year of showing I was productive, he was more accommodating," she says. "I started a couple of shorter days, then one day at home." At his suggestion, she currently works almost entirely from home.

Now, Rita's an expert of sorts on juggling alternative arrangements, if such a thing exists. She knows what it is to manage roles; she's a vice president at her firm and co-president of the middle school PTO. She finds work for women in HR roles. She herself works flexible hours mostly from home, and she is founder and chairperson of a special-interest group in the Boston area that supports women in alternative work arrangements called the Creative Work Options Network (CWON), which is now a part of the Northeast Human Resources Association.

"Our first session was almost like therapy," she says of the group's first meeting five years ago, a group that has grown significantly since. "You felt you didn't really fit with working moms, but you weren't completely stay-at-home either." The networking group, she says, initially gave women a chance to swap stories, to offer and receive advice, and to vent; it now also provides professional development and corporate education. From that and her own experiences, she's learned a lot.

Based on her knowledge, Rita's short answer to how you can best identify the right arrangement for you is this: "You have to evaluate your own needs and the needs of the business. You have to be flexible, be willing to work a lot at night. It's give and take," she says.

The long answer that she and others put forward? Read on and you'll find out.

Life is not predictable. Needs change. Your career does not have to follow a traditional path, slowly inching up a ladder, full-time and uninterrupted over the course of your working life. You can follow what more than one woman has told me is another path, a path that is neither the traditional career path that generations of men have forged nor the stay-at-home path that women once held. It is a path that falls somewhere between—a third way.

The fact is that more and more women are choosing that way. They are taking the brave step of charting paths of their own because the traditional path of full-time, fixed hours is one that often does not answer their ever-changing demands. They are starting businesses, working flexible hours, telecommuting, creating part-time professional roles, negotiating paid and/or extended maternity leave, and even temporarily stepping out of the workforce after the birth of a child.

But it hasn't always been this way. For decades, well-educated and skilled women have been dedicating their professional lives to crashing the glass ceiling. They've striven to achieve professional parity with men. They're broken into traditionally male-dominated fields, slowly edged up their pay, and attained more senior levels in greater numbers. But to succeed at that level, they also have had to operate on terms on which men have operated for years—namely, get ahead by working long hours consistently through their career. They've taken short maternity leaves; arranged others to care for the children when they're sick; consistently missed being home when children get on and/or off the bus; and worked traditional full-time schedules through most of their children's infancy, toddler, and school-age years. Many women have missed participating in significant areas of their children's lives, because they've had to follow a path that was created on the basis that the father worked at an office and the mother stayed home to care for the kids. There was no in between.

But a new generation of women is ushering in change. This change is evident in an emerging acceptance of flexible arrangements, an acceptance that 15 years ago was derided even by feminists as "The Mommy Track."[1] One woman in her 40s who was at a senior management level in her firm told me that years ago, when she proposed to her company that she work part-time, the women in the company felt she had in some way betrayed them. They felt, she said, that by proposing a part-time arrangement she was undermining what they had worked so hard to achieve. "People were freaked out," she says. "Let down." But she doesn't think that would happen now. "It's different," she says. More women, women just 10 years younger than she, are trailblazing a new path, one that allows for flexibility, she says. They're striving to make those arrangements work for them and for their employers. And as they succeed, they're beginning to reshape traditional perceptions of what a career or job can or should be.

Of course, many of the women who are succeeding in temporarily stepping out of the workforce, creating part-time professional roles, working flexible hours, and starting their own businesses are women who have well-honed skills and a good education. Many can afford to take on some of those roles, because they don't need benefits and can handle reduced pay and/or stalled career advancement. "I'm lucky. I get benefits through my spouse," was a refrain I heard over and over again in my interviews. These women (directly or indirectly) bartered for the flexibility they have.

But not all.

There Are Options

This section is intended to help you understand the nontraditional arrangements that women and, yes, even some brave men, are pursuing. Those include full-time and part-time and the variations within those—such as working for yourself, flexible hours, and working from home in part or in full. Some of these arrangements offer benefits, some do not. Some are better suited for certain industries or jobs. Some work better with certain skills sets or personality traits. But to make the arrangement work, each requires that you understand not only your own needs but also the nature of the job, your skills, and the standpoint of the supervisor and employer for whom you will work.

Unlike Small Children, Family-Friendly Arrangements Don't Climb into Your Lap

Of course, you will be misleading yourself if you think that you'll be able to move effortlessly onto this third way and stride gracefully ahead, briefcase in one hand and overstuffed, spine-damaging children's backpack in the other. For although the popularity of these arrangements is growing on the whole, the shift in perception is just beginning. Utilization rates are still relatively low.[2] Trade-offs are still palpable. Many people still do not pursue these arrangements because they feel they cannot afford to take on the trade-offs, whether those constitute a stalled career, less pay, or a diminished sense of self-worth. Some can't convince their employer that their proposed arrangement makes business sense. Some can't contend with unsupportive supervisors and colleagues.

This section will help you overcome those challenges. It will help you understand what these arrangements demand, so that you can make a business case for the arrangement you seek. It will help you win over skeptics, leverage your strengths, make well-considered concessions, and contend with people who believe that because you work on terms that are perceived as better than everyone else, that promotion, that raise, that opportunity is better deserved by someone else. It will help you manage the challenges that are inherent to family-friendly work. Can you work part-time and still meet your financial needs? Can you become self-employed and sacrifice employer-sponsored benefits? Can you bear the cost on your career, if not down the line, then in the short term?

It also will help you consider the relevance of your skills. Are your self-management skills conducive to working from home? Are the work-content skills you currently employ ones that can be applied in your desired arrangement? If not, can you reapply them in a way that makes them more viable? Are you willing to forgo using some of those skills so you can take on a role that's better suited to the arrangement you seek? If necessary, can you think about applying your transferable skills in other ways?

You may, of course, find that your family-friendly position bears little impact on the skills you use or your ability to fulfill your needs. You may work for a progressive-minded employer that does not penalize in any way those who hold alternative arrangements. You may get an "alternative arrangement" at a company where alternative arrangements are not alternative but mainstream. You may get benefits in a job where typically workers do not. But regardless, you need to understand alternative arrangements for what they are. You need to understand what they may offer and what they may not. And you need to understand how you, like the mothers in this book, can learn to control your career rather than let it control you.

Real Mother Recap

Now you've embarked on Step Three of this book. You're just past halfway. Lucky you! The point of this step is to give you an understanding of what each alternative arrangement demands and how well that arrangement jibes with your needs. Once you've done that, you can move onto the last step: Getting Family-Friendly Work. They you can do a little dance—and spiking the book is allowed.

10

Full-Time, Flexible

To be successful (with flexible scheduling), you have to be willing to be flexible.

–ROSE

ROSE

When Rose and I first set up our interview, my son was home with the flu. Don't be put off if my son answers the phone, I warned her. He's four, sick and needy. He didn't, but she was understanding all the same. "I'm a mother of three boys and am never put off by little ones in the background," she said.

Rose, who works full-time in brand development for an investment management company, knows what it's like to have little ones in the background. Prior to her current position, she worked as a consultant from home for five years. Two years ago, her current employer—through the recommendation of a friend— approached her about working for them. Rose knew it was the type of position that could afford some degree of flexibility; it didn't require that she manage people.

"Some positions, by the nature of the job, make it difficult for

the employer to be flexible," she says. This one, she knew, was not.
She also knew they wanted her, so she laid out her terms. "I was
very straightforward. [There was an] understanding set in the
interview process that I would need time to attend functions at
school, stay home with sick kids—and be supported. We receive almost 4 weeks paid time off which I use to take every Friday off in
the summer [and] for days when my children are home sick. Ad-
ditionally, they offer excellent benefits and flextime," she says.

But Rose also is realistic in what she asks. She knows, for example, the limits of flexibility. She knows that in the end she has to get
her job done and done well. She knows that when business is feeling
the crunch, as it has in the recent recession, she has to occasionally
forego some of that flexibility she so covets. "To be successful [with
flexible scheduling], you have to be willing to be flexible," she says.
She also knows the costs her decisions may bear on her career. The position she now holds, for example, is probably at the same level at
which she left another company 7 years ago to work for herself. "I
certainly didn't lose ground," she says, "but I didn't progress. Fortunately, I've been lucky to find work that is stimulating. I've still
been able to work with talented, interesting people."

In fact, perhaps above all else, Rose is realistic with what she can
expect out of herself, her work, and her home life. "Balance is key,"
she says. "I limit my activities outside work to those things I consider
essential—yoga class and book club. I try to choose commitments
that involve our family at church or in the community, things we
can do together." And lest I think it's all easy, that working a somewhat flexible schedule, raising three sons, and maintaining a
healthy relationship with her husband is effortless, she reminds me
again and again that it is not. "I don't want to paint a perfect picture," she says. "I was at the store shopping at 10:00 last night."

But through it all, she carries an awareness that so far life is
more or less working out. And that awareness—that ability to
transcend the small and keep sight of the larger, more important

aspects of her life—seems to permeate everything she says. "I don't have any regrets. I'm doing things that are important to me. I feel very fortunate that I've been able to create positions that work for me."

Depending on your earning capacity, need of financial support, or even professional objectives, full-time work may be what you need. Full-time work often means that salary, benefits, and time frame for career advancement remain intact. And for some mothers, among them perhaps the close to 40% of mothers in female-headed households with children under 18 who live in poverty, such criteria can be critical.[1] A full-time job that provides the security of a steady paycheck, benefits, and potential for career advancement is essential for many mothers, single or married. And some flexibility into the mix and full-time work may enable them to meet their needs—financial or professional—while still being available to their kids.

The Benefits to the Employee

But can full-time, flexible *really* be family-friendly? For many women, the answer is an unqualified yes. Flexibility for them is the defining factor in family-friendly work. "I think you have to take into consideration that when you have children so many things are out of your control," says one director of a career services department at a college in Nevada. Flexibility, she feels, gives parents the time they need to deal with issues as they arise without sacrificing their professional work. It allows Caroline, an oil analyst in Michigan, to attend school conferences. It allows Teresa, an e-commerce program manager in New York and single mother to an eight-year-old girl, to ferry her child to appointments and to attend school events. ("If it means that I can get only two hours of sleep at night, that's the cost," she says.) It gives Stephanie, that headhunter in

Massachusetts, time to volunteer at a school that she feels desperately needs parental involvement. It gives Cheryl, a project manager in South Carolina, peace of mind in knowing that she and her husband are earning enough to raise their two children without having to put them in after-school care for more than an hour each day. In fact, so coveted is flexibility that according to a 1998 study of women entrepreneurs by the nonprofit group Catalyst, 51% of women said flexibility was the top reason they had left their employers to start their own business.[2] And nearly 60% of women interviewed by that same research group (in a different study) said they would have left their jobs without the opportunity to work flexibly.[3]

Perhaps Hillary, a divorced mother from South Dakota, who works as a government lab technician and who really enjoys her "maxiflex" (no, not a new form of sanitary pad) schedule, puts it best. That maxiflex schedule has allowed her to change her start and finish times during the school year to 7:30 to 4:00 and to work a compressed schedule in the summer, with longer days and three-day weekends. She also has been able to schedule time to volunteer at her daughter's school. She says:

If you can find a job with flexible hours, grab it and hold onto it. I am very grateful that I am able to have a full-time job where I am mentally challenged every day and [can] still be as involved in school as most stay-at-home moms. I feel my daughter has gained a healthy outlook of work and home because she has been able to see me work and still be an involved parent. I haven't had to experience guilt for missing anything, and yet I didn't have to sacrifice my career in the process. I have been able to take advantage of continuing education in the summers when she's visiting her dad so I still have professional development for future job opportunities. I have three-day weekends all summer long to spend with her, and still perform at acceptable levels of work. I know all too well how lucky I've been and realize that most women are not as fortunate.

Why Employers Offer It

Given statements like these, is it any wonder that employers offer flexible scheduling? Provided the employee can still get the job done, full-time flexible scheduling is a benefit that employers may be able to provide at no real cost to them. Many, as a result, do just that. One study found that some 88% of companies with 100 or more employees allowed workers to take time off to attend school and child-care functions.[4] "We may not be able to pay a lot, but we can hook them with flexibility," says that analyst and human resource manager at the Michigan-based petrochemicals research firm. In fact, according to a 1999 report by the U.S. Bureau of Labor Statistics, more than a quarter of full-time wage and salary workers in 1997 had flexible work schedules on their principal job. Married workers with children under six years old lead the charge.[5]

Who Gets It

Of course, flexible schedules are more common among some professions than others. Executives, administrators, managers, and salespeople more commonly have flexible schedules than production workers, repairwomen, operators, or laborers. Likewise, the proportion of workers with flexible schedules is also higher in service-producing industries than goods-producing ones.[6] For example: while one in nine machine operators has a flexible daily work schedule, as many as three in five natural or mathematical scientists, lawyers, and sales representatives have such schedules.[7] Yes, some factories and other goods-producing companies are beginning to try to introduce flextime into their organizations by cross-training employees to handle tasks while employees are out. But flexible hours often are not seen as practical or cost-effective for employees who have to be on site—time card punched—to get their work done. If the nature of the job dictates that it begin and end at set times (as is the case with policework, firefighting, and many jobs in manufacturing) flexible scheduling can be rare.

Flexible schedules are also more common among those who are experienced with highly desirable skills. Executives, for example, are more likely to have flexible work hours than anyone else.[8] Why? It's reasonable to assume that if you have been working at a company for a while and have a very strong set of skills, you're probably more likely to get an alternative arrangement than someone else. You've got the leverage others don't.

What Are the Possible Options?

Like most arrangements, full-time flexibility is not anything like the old maternity dresses—one size does not fit all. It comes in varied forms, depending on the demands of your job and the policies of your employer. Some break it down into two types of arrangements: "gliding days" and "flextime." Gliding days require a specified number of hours of work each day and are built around established core hours with varying start and finish times. Flextime allows employees to choose the number of hours they wish to work each day or each week and to use credit or compensatory time based on overtime hours they've worked. Another way to break those policies down is like this:

- **Flextime:** Employees choose starting and ending hours but usually must be at work during core hours when most employees are present. Flextime with a two-hour band (e.g., the ability to arrive at work between 7:00 and 9:00 A.M.) is twice as prevalent as flextime with a four-hour band.[9]

- **Flexible Week:** A variation on the standard workday or work-week. Variations include compressed workweeks (fewer but longer days over a one- or two-week period), extended work-weeks (shorter days in a six-day week), or some variation of either of the above. Regardless, the average hours worked will be 37 to 40 a week or whatever the standard workweek is within the company. Working four 10-hour days a week tends to be more popular than 80 hours over nine days.[10]

- **Flexible Day:** For want of any widely used term, I call an arrangement flexible day when employees are allowed to interrupt their workday to attend to personal matters on the condition that their work still gets done. This arrangement may exist as part of a flextime or flexible week policy or on its own. It may be written policy, but more likely it will not be on the books. Employees with this flexibility can leave at the supervisor's or their discretion. It's the most common form of flexibility. This arrangement obviously is most effective for parents when the place of work is close to home.

Some employers will offer these policies formally; some will not have the policies written down at all. No matter how you slice it, the substance is the same. These arrangements give you the ability to change your hours to varying extents to meet outside demands but still work full-time.

Is Flexible Scheduling Right for You?

Time to get out that bookmark again. Look first, if you will, at your parenting needs. Ask yourself to what extent you feel you need to be present in your children's lives to maintain a strong and sustaining relationship. If you feel that you will be able to organize your life to work 40 or more hours a week and still sustain that relationship by being present in your child's life at select times, flexible scheduling may work for you.

This arrangement also might be important if you have particular financial needs. If you need employer-sponsored benefits or to bring in your full earning capacity to meet your income needs, this may be the most desirable of family-friendly arrangements for you. Some suggest that flexible, full-time schedules can bear an impact on pay or rate of advancement, but there's little evidence to support that view. Regardless, it probably won't derail either, if managed well.

Now look at your strengths. These are very important. Why? Because if you pursue flexible scheduling, you must realize that a flexible schedule does not take you off the hook from getting the job done well. You are still going to have to work as hard and are probably not going to be working any *less*. The managing human resource professional at one marketing company that operates on the mantra "minimal adult supervision" notes, "We give employees flexibility to come and go as they please. As long as [they] perform, there's no issue."

So the first thing you want to make sure of is that your work-content skills are strong enough to support the schedule you set up. If you come into the office before everyone else, do you have the capability to get some of your work done alone? Do you have the self-management skills to support that? Are you capable of getting the work done given the schedule you desire?

Think, too, about the type of work-content skills you have. Where are they best applied? You're clearly better off if those skills pertain to jobs that don't have set start and finish times and that are not in the goods-producing industry. So if your work-content skills best apply to being a firefighter, it's probably not realistic to expect you can use those skills to get a flexible schedule in that role. Exceptions exist, such as a factory worker who worked with her team to find flexible hours by allowing team members to cover for one another so that they could meet family demands, but such instances

Shift Work and Nonstandard Hours

As the demand for weekend and non-daytime workers grows in what is increasingly becoming a 24/7 economy, the number of mothers and fathers working opposite hours, or "split-shift couples" as they're now commonly called, is on the rise. As a result, stories abound of Mom and Dad playing tag team so they can meet the demands of the kids and still earn the wages and benefits they need. For the dual-income family, split-shift parenting almost seems a family-friendly option in itself.

Almost.

Split-shift parenting that results from staggered shift work and/or nonstandard hours can save money on child care and give one parent more time with their children, depending on the time of the shift and the age of the children. But studies also suggest that split-shift parenting can have detrimental effects on home life in far-reaching ways. Not only do families miss out on having two parents around in the evening when families often dine together and children need help with their homework, but night shifts can take a serious toll on a parent's rest, health, and general outlook on life. These all contribute to a home environment that for many is not an ideal way to structure family life.

Once more, split-shift parenting can seriously affect a marriage. Harriet Presser, a professor at the University of Maryland, has extensively studied nonstandard work schedules. When she focused on male and female shift workers, she found that fathers married less than five years and working the night shift were six times more likely to become separated or divorced than those working days. Among mothers married more than five years, working nights increased the odds of separation or divorce by three times.[*]

Still, these facts don't change the fact that some people to whom I spoke feel their ability to work at night and do split-shift parenting makes their work more manageable given their home demands. But on looking more thoroughly, I saw those arrangements usually came with flexibility. These women had the choice of when and to what extent they worked or had found ways to get colleagues to trade shifts to cover home demands. Says one registered nurse: "My new nurse manager let me choose the number of hours I wanted to work per week as well as the shifts. I'm a part-timer. I work every other weekend, and when I work a 3 to 11 [shift], my husband comes home early and works the remainder of his day from home. I have the best of both worlds."

In fact, shift work is not unlike other forms of traditional work. Make it more accommodating, through better child care, compressed work weeks, part-time work, or cross-training that allows for some degree of flexible days, and it too becomes more family-friendly. The challenge for shift workers—who tend to need family-friendly benefits the most but get it the least—is finding employers who can do just that.

*Harriet B. Presser, "Nonstandard Work Schedules and Marital Instability," Journal of Marriage and Family 62, no. 1:93–110.

are rare. If flexibility is important to you, you're probably going to have to think about other ways in which you can apply those same skills, something I'll get into in later chapters of this book.

Also, don't assume that just because an occupation has a relatively high proportion of flexible workers that it is necessarily family-friendly. A high percentage of farmers, for example, may have flexible schedules, but many also work more than 45 hours per week.[11] In fact, many jobs with flexible hours have shifts that are long, irregular, and/or are scheduled at nonstandard times (such as at night).[12] On the other hand, most professional, administrative, supervisory, and secretarial jobs, for example, tend to have a more stable, predictable week, something that will probably be easier to manage when you're simultaneously trying to manage kids.

What Kind of Schedule Is Best for You

If you do decide that your skills and needs match up with the flexible, full-time arrangement, your next step is to consider what kind of schedule might work for you. Which form of flexibility—flextime (altered start and finish times), flexible weeks (compressed work-weeks or extended weeks), flexible days, or some combination of those—is best for you and your child? If you have a toddler who goes to school in the morning and takes afternoon naps, perhaps you want to start your day late and return in early evening. If you have an adolescent, perhaps you want to leave early and be home early so you can greet her when she gets back from school in the afternoons. If you have an elementary-school student and participating in the school is important to you, perhaps you want time off in the day, an arrangement that obviously works best if your place of work is near where your children go to school.

Realize, of course, that a full-time flexible schedule probably will work better if your child's other parent is able to share child-care responsibilities owing to flexibility in his or her work arrangement (children, studies show, do better with both parents involved on a daily basis in their lives). If you're interested in learning more about this shared care concept, visit www.thirdpath.org. Also be honest with yourself. If your children are not yet in school and you have a desire to be home with them, don't fool yourself into thinking that flexible scheduling will give you that time. You are still working full-time. Wanting to be home, to be a parent who spends a lot of time with her child, is a need in itself. If your financial situation allows you to work less, don't rule it out simply because you feel you *ought* to work full-time.

Last, don't underestimate the importance of child care. You want first and foremost to make sure your child gets quality care. If your flexible arrangement does not allow that—your children are in a day care that has rigid hours—don't make that move until you have found an alternative that is equally as good. Your child must have good child care when you're not there.

Now look at your bookmark again. You'll note that under "Arrangement I Want," "Flexibility" and "Full-time" are listed sep-

How to Make Flexible Hours Work

FIND COVERAGE AT HOME

If you want to take time off to volunteer at school, you'll still be expected to get the job done—even if it means working late, on weekends, or in the middle of the night. Make sure you have the flexibility to support that arrangement on the home front, particularly when it comes to child care. If you're married or in a relationship, get your partner or spouse on board. You'll *both* have to make it work. If your home situation is one that cannot well accommodate changes in schedules, flexibility may not be right for you.

FIND COVERAGE AT WORK

You need to make sure the systems are in place to manage what's important while you're not there. If your job is time-sensitive or needs 24-hour coverage, you may have to cross-train, be willing to interrupt your time off, or work out a way for someone to be there. "Cross-train colleagues to help out when you might feel stressed by leaving," one software support specialist points out. If you can't get coverage, you may have to put off proposing a flexible arrangement until the systems are in place to cope.

BE FLEXIBLE YOURSELF

Flexibility is never guaranteed. If supervisors or colleagues make allowances for you, they will sometimes expect you to make allowances for them. That may mean occasionally staying late, attending a meeting for which you hadn't planned, reciprocating a favor by covering for a colleague or supervisor when they step out. Says one mother who works for a petrochemicals company: "Nine/80 [working 80 hours over a nine-day period] is widely practiced in our company. However, there is an understanding that it is not guaranteed. If something comes up with work, you may have to reschedule or skip that 9/80." Make sure you feel comfortable occasionally missing that day off or time away you had planned. If that time away is something you absolutely *cannot* miss, you may need something else, like some form of leave.

SET BOUNDARIES AT WORK

Setting boundaries is important if you want to successfully manage home and work. You can facilitate that by understanding your job and prioritizing the tasks and responsibilities it brings. By knowing, for example, what your boss and you perceive to be your most important responsibilities, you can focus on what's important in your job, setting boundaries as to what you will do, and proposing to allocate where you can. If you've established that you need to leave at 5:30 each day, is that unscheduled 6:00 meeting *really* necessary for you to attend? If you've established that you don't have to travel for your job, make sure you can say no if it's not essential to your work. If your responsibilities and workload grow or change and those boundaries prove too difficult to maintain, reassess. If you're someone who can't say no, flexible, full-time work is going to be hard for you.

SET BOUNDARIES AT HOME

The same holds true at home. Decide what's most important to you in your work as a mother, woman, and even—if applicable—wife, and try to stick to it. Don't be afraid to delegate where you can. And just as you need to be available to the business when you're at work, try to be present for your family when you're home. Don't let work color your home life. Again, if you're someone who can't say no, flexible, full-time work is going to be hard for you on the home front as well.

ESTABLISH GOOD COMMUNICATION AT WORK AND HOME

Keep your work colleagues abreast of your schedule and your boundaries. If they're having a meeting when you're not in, send an e-mail reminding them you'll be out and asking if they could leave a copy of the report on your desk. Post your schedule on your office door, in the computer system, at your desk, on the refrigerator, in your partner's briefcase. Be sure people who need to know, know your whereabouts. Keep the lines of communication as open as you can. If you need to say no to a project or task that falls outside your responsibilities, be sure you let that colleagues know in a way that shows you have the interest of the business at heart. If someone at work oversteps boundaries you've set, let them know that won't work, suggesting, if possible, an alternative instead. "I can't talk about business tonight, how about tomorrow morning first thing?" If a child wants you to attend an event that you can't, do the same. As you do this, be sensitive to demands that not being at work or at home may place on somebody else. While you don't have to lick the floor, don't forget to say thanks. If you are not a good communicator, work on that first.

SEEK OUT SUPPORT AT WORK AND HOME

To really thrive at work or home, you need support. If your supervisor is among those cheerleaders, you're even better off. Says Hillary, that divorced mother of one teenager from South Dakota. "My supervisor was a close friend before she was promoted to her position. She said as long as the work is done and I'm working the required hours, she isn't going to micromanage my schedule. She has always been supportive of my involvement at the school." If you don't have a strong supporter at work, strive for that.

The same holds true at home. Yon need people who have the interests of you and your children at heart, who can give you the information you need when you're not there, who can step in when you need help. Says one mother about managing home life while working, "If it weren't for my friends, I wouldn't have been able to do it." If you don't have strong support at home, build that.

DON'T BE AFRAID TO SELF-PROMOTE

When someone makes a halfhearted jibe that you weren't around, make a halfhearted jibe back: "Missed you this morning at 7:00 as well." The occasional e-mail sent while you're working at night or on the weekend isn't a bad thing either. You want to let it be known that you still took the time to get the work done and that you did it well. Don't let the fact that you're not at the office set you back. If you don't have the courage to reply, to stand up for yourself, find it.

REVIEW AND ASSESS

Once you have your arrangement in place, don't forget to review and assess it. Set up regular reviews with your supervisor. Set these more frequently at first—perhaps after the first two months—less frequently once the arrangement has been in place for a while. Be willing to discuss changing or altering your approach if you or your employer feels that needs aren't being met.

arately. If you need full-time and think a flexible schedule will work for you based on your strengths and needs, check both. If you feel full-time is not for you, but some other form of flexible hours may be, just check off flexible. Your next step will be to consider how you can secure and manage that arrangement. Above are some tips on managing flexible schedules. After you read them, you are welcome to skip to Step Four on securing family-friendly work, if you feel you've identified the arrangement you want.

Real Mother Recap

Now I hope you've ascertained whether a full-time, flexible schedule might meet the needs of you and your family. You understand that flexible schedules are the most common type of nontraditional arrangement that employers offer, and that flexibility is what employees most want. You understand that some jobs—such as those that do not have set start and finish times—are better positioned to take advantage of flexible scheduling, just as some highly skilled people—such as executives—are better positioned to take advantage of that scheduling. You understand that strong support systems, good communication skills, clearly defined boundaries, flexibility on all sides, and an employer who embraces flexible scheduling all help make that arrangement work. And you understand that no matter how ideal the arrangement may seem, if it doesn't meet the needs or desires of you and your family, it will never be entirely family-friendly to you.

If you need more information: visit the Center for Work and Family Balance (www.workandfamily.org) or check out BlueSuitMom.com (www.bluesuitmom.com). And don't forget to use your own network—professional association or otherwise—to research how well flexible work arrangements are implemented in your industry.

11

Telecommuting

It's how we get the top candidates.

—co-owner of a PR company
on why telecommuting makes sense for her bottom line

SOMEWHERE IN MANHATTAN

It's 11:00 A.M. on a Thursday, and eight women—many of them mothers—and one man are sitting in a rented room trying to organize another one of their company's face-to-face meetings.

"It's got to get done," says the meeting's chair, a mother of two and company co-founder. "It's like spring cleaning. You've hired the baby-sitter, you've handed your husband the cleanser. It's time."

But where and exactly when? This group of employees lives and works from home offices that are scattered across New England. Getting together is no small task. If the meeting is going to be held in Connecticut, the woman at the opposite end of the table would please like it to coincide with her trip to visit her sister nearby. ("Why not ask?" she says with a bemused shrug.) The woman to the left has a conflicting play rehearsal ("I've got a husband, a son—life's crazy," she later confides while handing out the program of her upcoming off-Broadway play). The man doesn't even think the meeting necessary ("Are you crazy?" says the shut-him-down glares of his co-workers). Ultimately, the meeting's chair and company boss, Isadora, sets the date and venue. "My place. We can spread out in the kitchen, my office, even the dining room if we have to."

With annual revenue just shy of $2 million the previous year and a growing list of heavyweight clients, this telecommuting company—run by a mom and a dad—is proving that companies can be family-friendly—to an extent.

Here, people aren't afraid to voice personal conflicts or use domestic metaphors. They get benefits, good clients, and stimulating work. They are privy to home occurrences that many working moms miss. They know if the child-care giver is good or if their adolescent is acting out after school. They're home if an emergency strikes. They have flexible schedules and can take a minute to put the roast in the oven, as long as the work gets done. Even the boss ducks out to attend a parent–teacher conference or occasionally to drop a child off at school. "We're all grown-ups," she says.

But both the company and its employees have a set of realities with which they have to cope. If, for example, you're a mom and want to work part-time, forget it. This public relations company has stopped hiring part-time employees, because the owners feel that in a client-services business, people need to be accessible five days a week. Want to look after your child yourself while you work? No, again. This work demands professionalism, and it's too difficult to be professional while your child demands juice, books, and games. Social interaction? You'll get relatively little of it here; your home office can be a pretty isolating place. On-the-job training? Sorry, you won't get much of that either. To work on these terms, you have to be self-sufficient and highly skilled with a strong knowledge base. You can't learn by looking over the shoulder of a colleague, because that colleague works miles away.

Yes, this company just may be trying to make the corporate world a better place, but it's also got its own self-interest at stake. This is business, and business comes first.

Telecommuting—being able to work somewhere other than the office—may seem like a privilege. It may seem like something granted out of a company's good will to employees who have earned the reward—think again.

Why Employers Offer It

Telecommuting, like other family-friendly arrangements, has to be in the interest of the business first. If a small company sets up an entirely telecommuting staff, the owners are probably not doing it primarily to make the world a better place, striving to do their part to bring car emissions down. They've got a business to run and for some reason—whether to lower real-estate costs, attract talent, increase productivity, lower absenteeism, engender employee loyalty, raise morale, reduce turnover, or even generate press—they've decided that the move will benefit the company more than it costs.

Many employers clearly see those benefits. While there is conflicting data as to how many people work from home, the numbers are relatively high. The U.S. Department of Labor's suggests that some 13 to 19 million workers telework today.[1] The International Telework Association and Council, puts that number around 28 million or 1 in 5 workers over the age of 18.[2] The reason for the discrepancy is that *teleworking* is a vague term. Some people work from home and don't get paid for that work. Some people work from home informally and are paid but not specifically for "working at home." Some people work in satellite centers, on the road, or in their own businesses from home. All these can be family-friendly in their way. "Drop-in" centers or satellite centers, for example, may be family-friendly to those who don't want to commute but who need access to office equipment, peers, or information that a home office can't provide. But working from home for pay is probably the most desired form of telecommuting and, therefore, the one I address here.

The Benefits to the Employee

Why is it so popular? One accountant in a small firm in Nevada puts the benefit this way: "Working from home has been a huge help in juggling family demands."

In fact, telecommuting from home can help mothers juggle in numerous ways. Because their children are at their office step, many mothers say time they would have wasted commuting is spent with their children instead. Thanks to the fact that they are at home, they often can eke out additional time as well. That one-hour lunch in which a commute home would hardly be worth the trip suddenly takes on new significance. One single mother and account-support coordinator from Montana, for example, breaks up her lunch hour into two 30-minute breaks. She eats lunch and showers in the first half-hour and uses the other 30-minute break either to greet her son at the bus or to pick him up from his activity.

In addition, there's the benefit of being in close proximity to your children, even if you're not with them. You can hear if that new care giver speaks lovingly to your children. You can greet your adolescent child after school or see whether your toddler is unhappy during the day. You're nearby if your child cuts his face. You have proximity and a peace of mind that you might otherwise lack.

You also may get a degree of flexibility that is harder to have when working on-site. "I found it much more stressful to work part-time at an office," one translator from Phoenix told me. "It seemed I often had to call to change my schedule due to family demands. Working at home on my own time means I can do my work on a schedule that works." For by working from home, you often *can* pop out to tend to a domestic matter "as long as the work gets done," a refrain I heard among telecommuters over and over again.

Who Gets It

Of course, as with other nontraditional arrangements, not everyone gets access to telecommuting arrangements. The first reason being that some jobs simply can't be done from anywhere but the office. Many jobs that require face-to-face interaction with customers or colleagues are not well suited for telecommuting arrangements. Jobs that require on-site work with machines, such as factory jobs, don't work well either. So what does work? According to a report by the Department of Labor, telework is best suited to jobs that are information-based, portable, and predictable or that demand a high degree of privacy and concentration.[3] Judging by where the highest concentration of paid teleworkers fall, managerial, professional, and sales occupations often fit that bill.[4]

Susan Seitel, president of the Work & Family Connection, a service that tracks information on work and life initiatives, lists the following as possible telecommuting jobs:[5]

- Accountants
- Analysts
- Architects
- Catalog agents
- Computer programmers
- Customer service representatives
- Data entry operators
- Engineers
- Lawyers
- Managers
- Packaging designers
- Personnel specialists

- Program planners
- Public relations
- Professionals
- Sales representatives
- Systems analysts

- Technical writers
- Telemarketing personnel
- Telephone sales
- Travel agents
- Word processors

If you go on the basis that information-based jobs are more conducive to at-home telecommuting, you can add consultants, editors, graphic designers, journalists, and other occupations that rely on information to the mix. Of course, jobs that rely on sophisticated and expensive equipment to provide that information may not work in telecommuting arrangements. One financial analyst for a large investment bank in Chicago says that telecommuting for her job does not make sense. She needs constant and up-to-date access to expensive information systems that are best used at work, not at home. But some do arrange partial telecommuting in such situations by doing job tasks at home that do not rely on those systems. In fact, most telecommuting arrangements are not five days a week; one or two days is more common, according to the Department of Labor.[6]

As with other nontraditional arrangements, telecommuters also tend to be in mid-level or senior positions. The Department of Labor notes that teleworking is increasingly moving toward existing at all levels of employment, but it's not there in great numbers yet. Why? The first reason is that many of those jobs that can be done from home are, by their nature, more senior. A receptionist or blue-collar worker needs to be on-site. The same holds true for a training position, or more junior position, as employees often need to be on-site to learn. Second, the more senior you are, the more likely you are going to be able to convince your employer that you can get the job done, despite your altered terms. And given the perceived challenges that telecommuting presents, that leverage can be key.

Among the smaller of those challenges can be costs. If the company decides to foot the bill, setting up a home office can ring the company register up thousands of dollars per telecommuter. Computers, faxes, modems, computer security, and phone lines with forwarding capability all add up. That's not to mention the cost in time and repair when your system malfunctions—repair that is usually easier and more efficient if it's on-site. But these costs are not the issue for most. Many small companies don't pay to set up home offices and even if companies do pay, the savings in real-estate costs can outweigh setup costs.

The real hurdle for companies that have jobs that theoretically *could* be done from home is more intangible than that. There's a supervisor or employer's fear that if she allows one person to telecommute, everyone will want to, like sheep. But there's also the even larger fear that if an employer changes the way work is done at a company, the business may suffer. Teams and organizations won't sit together as they once did. Work won't be overseen to the same extent. Employees won't be able to stop by a cubicle, drop a memo on a desk, sit around a table and brainstorm until lunch. The nature of communication and interaction will inevitably—even if only to a small extent—change, becoming more premeditated and formal than an open-plan, cubicle-strewn office allows. The bang that you get from crashing 10 heads together won't be heard. Says Cloe, creative director at a marketing company and mother to two children:

In this business, it's easy to produce work from home. What is missing is the collaboration and input that happens when you're in the office. Being part of a team is very important to the creative process and to the culture of a small company.

These fears are no doubt part of the reason that utilization rates for telecommuting are so low at many organizations, as low as 6% in one study.[7]

But there's one more factor behind the low rates of utilization. Some people simply don't feel that telecommuting is right for them. Among the women I interviewed, several decided just that. For them, telecommuting blurred the line between home and work. They couldn't escape the fact that "my work is always there, waiting," as one woman says, or that their children were doing the same. These women had trouble keeping the two apart. Says that woman from Texas who works in the finance department of a petroleum company: "I actually did telecommute for two months when coming back from family leave. Personally, I did not like it and felt that there was a blurring between my work and personal life." She now works a compressed schedule—nine longer days over a two-week period—and is much happier.

Some people also yearn for the stimulation and social interaction that a busy work environment provides. A lone chair and silent room is not what they want. They may even feel they work better when they have people against whom they can bounce off ideas, even if only casually in a stairwell or at lunch. Says Marina, a management consultant who decided after a short stint that telecommuting was not for her, "I was getting tired of working from home. What I enjoyed about work was social and working in a team setting. I loved working in a collaborative fashion. I didn't feel like I was learning as much. I'm better at bringing people's ideas together."

Last, depending on how it's managed, telecommuting can mean sacrificing supervisory roles and missing out on opportunities for advancement—the classic case of out of sight, out of mind that many employees fear. "That's fine for me," said one mother in public relations, whose priority at the moment is her children not her career. But some don't want to give that up.

Is Telecommuting Right for You?

All these factors beg one question: Is telecommuting right for you? As you consider that question, get out your bookmark again. Look first at your parenting needs. Do you feel the flexibility and proximity of telecommuting will help you better meet your children's needs? Could you telecommute part or all of your work time and attend to the demands you've listed? How often would you need to work from home to do that? Is there a time of day or week that you and your family would be best served if you were working at home? Would that give you a peace of mind that you don't currently have and allow you to bring more to parenting? It's not coincidence, by the way, that paid telecommuting work is most common among parents with children under the age of 6.[8] Proximity can mean a lot.

Consider, too, your financial and professional needs. Do you need to be in an office to satisfy your professional needs? Are you at a stage of your career or your employment where you really need to be on-site learning as much as you can? Can you get the power or recognition that you need if you do work from home? Do you need to be getting as many pay raises as you can? Is social interaction very important to you?

As you think about these needs, think also about the number of days you'd like to telecommute. Remember one or two days a week is most common. Ask yourself what kind of impact do you think one or two days would have to better support your relationship with your children.

Now think about your skills. These are key when it comes to telecommuting. Do you have strong work-content skills that you can do from home? If, for example, you want a job writing press releases from home, do you have experience writing them? Simply having the transferable skill of writing may not be good enough. Employers need to know your work-content skills are strong enough to get the job done on your own. Remember Isadora, who heads that PR telecommuting company? She hires only senior people with specific experience in their field. Why? Well, if you're alone at home, you're not going to learn by looking over a colleague's shoulder. If you don't have the right type of work-content skills, do you have transferable skills or knowledge areas that you could apply to jobs or tasks that are "information-based, portable, and predictable or that demand a high degree of privacy and concentration?" Would you have to learn new work-content skills in the process and could you do that at home or in a classroom or would you have to first work on-site?

Also look at your self-management skills. What kind of a worker are you? Would you work well at home? Would you enjoy it? Would you come away being able to engage with your children positively? Or would work at home get you down? Remember that not everyone is well suited to telecommute. You won't have anyone reminding you that the job has to get done. You won't have the buzz of a newsroom or a trading floor. You won't have the repartee that a busy office can provide. To do it well, you need self-management skills that include time management, an ability to work independently, and a large degree of initiative. Does this seem like you?

If You Feel Telecommuting Is Right for You

If after looking at your skills and your needs, you feel in your heart that telecommuting—at some level—might be for you, you will need to consider how you can manage that arrangement to your best advantage and to the best advantage of your employer. When you propose a work arrangement to an employer, you'll need to break down your job or prospective job into tasks and responsibilities that can be done at home or during off-hours, a process you will undertake in the last section of this book. In the meantime, I've

How to Make Telecommuting Work

YOU HAVE TO DELIVER

As a telecommuter, you will be under pressure to show that you can and will deliver. If you're at home, no one really knows what exactly you do all day. Are you really working or are you kicking around that inflatable ball with the blow-up frog inside it with the kids? To avoid room for doubt, establish clear deliverables and methods of evaluation with your supervisor. If you can't do a task from home, be sure that task still gets done, either by allocating it to someone or arranging a time you can come into the office and do it yourself. If you must, do as Samantha says at the beginning of the book—"under promise and over deliver."

BE PROFESSIONAL

Be as professional as you can, not just with clients but with colleagues as well. Some might resent the fact that you work from home, and you don't want to give them reason to call into question your arrangement. Have the right systems in place. Install a dedicated phone line. Get fax capability. If you are using the Internet in any way, try to get a high-speed connection. Be sure you have the office supplies you need, like a stapler and postage. If working for a small company, be prepared to buy your own equipment and be sure it's compatible with the office system. If you go out, make sure colleagues know where they can reach you. Cell phones are not always reliable, as they lose their signal—so be sure you check your messages frequently. Get a pager if you must. Set up an e-mail reply if you're gone from the office for more than a couple of hours. Don't broadcast the fact that you work at home. Isadora, the head of a telecommuting company, recommends: "Don't even say you're home. Don't make it an issue. If you're doing your job and doing it well, why should it matter?" Perhaps most important of all, make sure you are not trying to work and care for the kids at the same time. If you are working and your children need supervision, get child care!

DEFINE YOUR WORKSPACE—KEEPING KIDS (AND THE PARTNER!) OUT

At a symposium for telecommuting put together by the Department of Labor, one participant reportedly said that when parents work at home, fathers see children as a "temptation" and mothers seem them as a "responsibility."[9] It's much easier to say no to temptation than to responsibility. But you must. Clients—and for that matter colleagues—don't want to hear kids screaming in the back. Don your "I'm-working" hat, lock the door, go out the door and sneak back, do what you must to establish that you are at work. Make sure you and your children know that your space is for uninterrupted work. One magazine editor who telecommutes in the summer two days a week defines it this way: "An at-home worker needs a space, however small, that is sacred and time frames, however small, that are sacred. Sacred in the worker's mind and in the minds of his or her family members." Family members include your partner. Just because you are working from home does not mean that you are available for nonemergency interruptions.

MAINTAIN YOUR NETWORK AND YOUR CONNECTION TO WORK

Marianne is a writer who writes marketing materials. She works most days, 8:00 to 2:00 from home while her four children are in school. But one day a week she goes into the office all day. Why? To stay in touch. "If I'm gone from the environment, I lose track of how they talk about their work, what they provide to their customers, what opportunities they have to design new products or change their message to market their products in a different way." In short, staying connected means she performs better.

You need people to advocate for you, support you, send work your way. If you're not bumping into those people every day, work harder to keep yourself in their radar. Schedule regular face-to-face meetings, regular office hours, regular telephone calls, and teleconference meetings. Attend weekly meetings and periodic formal or informal gatherings. E-mail as necessary. Respond quickly when someone calls. And be sure you convey to your supervisor what you're doing and where you are.

DON'T BE AFRAID TO SELF-PROMOTE

Take advantage of opportunities to show that you're getting the job done and doing it well. If you receive backhanded remarks, point out your value. "Sorry, I forgot you, but I never see you." "That's because I'm working so hard making sure your presentation goes well." If you don't have the courage to reply, to stand up for yourself, find it. Don't let people lose sight of your value.

REVIEW AND ASSESS

Once you have your arrangement in place, don't forget to regularly review and assess it. Set up regular reviews with your supervisor. Set these more frequently at first—perhaps after the first two months—less frequently once the arrangement has been in place for a while. Be willing to discuss changing or altering your approach if you or your employer feels that business needs are not being met.

provided some tips on managing telecommuting work. After reading it, if you feel that a full-time telecommuting arrangement is right for you, check "Full-time" and "Telecommuting" on your bookmark and move on to Step Four. If you think telecommuting may be right for you but not full-time, just check "Telecommuting."

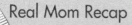

Real Mom Recap

You should have an idea now of what telecommuting is, what jobs are best positioned to take advantage of it, and what to consider if you want to make it work. You should also know that—as ideal as it may sound—it is not for everyone. To be successful at it, you have to be willing to work on your own, achieve clearly set objectives, be very professional and disciplined about your work, and strive hard to produce. You also have to put more effort against staying connected to the world of work outside your office. But if you can do all that, you may find the arrangement worth the effort it takes.

If you need more information: the Department of Labor provides good information on teleworking (www.dol.gov/asp/telework). You can also check out the International Telework Association Council (www. workingfromanywhere.org) or try *The Online Magazine for Work at Home Moms* (www.wahm.com).

12

Part-Time Work

No one ever had a discussion about lifestyle when I was young. I grew up in that era when we could do whatever we wanted and somehow it would all work out.

—JULIA

JULIA

"My reaction to motherhood was totally unanticipated. I never fantasized about motherhood and suburbia and station wagons. I always assumed I had a high-powered career and somehow it would all fit. Then I had Oliver and I really flipped about him. I had had a string of miscarriages, which I'm sure contributed to my reaction. I knew, at that point, I was not going to be able to work full-time. Full-time in medicine never means 40 hours."

So begins Julia, a pediatrician and mother to two elementary-school-aged children. She now works 20 hours a week at a medical clinic, an arrangement that she believes can be difficult to secure in many fields of medicine because of the demands and the mind-set of those who work within it. "We're still brainwashed in a way in medicine to believe it needs to be consuming, a passion," she says.

When she moved out to suburbia, however, she was determined not to fall into working long hours each week. She sent out job search letters to a range of hospitals and clinics, pointing to her experience and education. In subsequent discussions, she was clear on the number of hours she wanted to work. Her current employer accepted those in stride.

"He is lovely, evolved, understanding," she says. "He had a wife who took off eight years to care for their children. He saw himself as a child advocate who really believed that it was best for a mother to be around." He made her an offer, and—as she put it—she "stepped off the prestige track, off the fast track" and took the job.

The change of direction was a struggle for Julia in some respects. She'd never been comfortable with free time, "smelling the roses" as she says. She had excelled academically, worked hard to get into the medical school of her choice. Now she was giving up the prestige and recognition of what she could achieve for the ability to be home a good portion of the week.

"No one ever had a discussion about lifestyle when I was young. I grew up in that era when we could do whatever we wanted and somehow it would all work out. Sometimes, I feel like an anti-feminist. [When I first got here], sometimes I'd go up and down the aisles of the grocery store with tears in my eyes and think, how did I get here?"

But overall, she's happy with the choices she's made. "You need to be clear on what you need to do," she says. "If I hadn't waited five years to have a child I might not have been willing to give up what I did." But, she says, "I had this amazing child who opened my eyes to things."

So what will she tell her children when it comes to their careers? "I wish my children will think about this more, about how this will all fit in. I would never give the message that you can do it all."

Contrary to popular belief, part-time is making headway in today's workplace and women are leading the way. Yes, the number of women choosing part-time work is no longer growing. But whereas 20 years ago it may have been difficult to find people in a professional capacity who worked part-time, now it's estimated that 10% or more of professional workers choose that route.[1] And guess what? Those professionals and managers are much more likely to be women than men.[2] In fact, women still have a much greater chance of working part-time than men, with about a quarter of women being part-time as opposed to about a tenth of men.[3]

As I've said before, about one third of women managers will work part-time at some point of their career and the median age of those part-timers is 40.9, when women are in the midst of family responsibilities. But *child care* per se doesn't explain it all. For many of these women, time they gain at home is a worthwhile end in itself. That time can provide an opportunity to be more abreast of their children's lives, to physically care for their children more, to better manage the often conflicting demands of home and work. It gives them, many say, more balance in their lives, answering a need to be with their children, a need that many felt deeper than they had anticipated before they had kids. "I never knew how pervasive that need was going to be," says Hayley, who now works part-time for a small intellectual property development firm.

Yes, they concede, working part-time has real, tangible trade-offs, trade-offs that can leave women awake at night wondering about the decisions they've made, wondering, as Julia puts it, whether they are anti-feminists. But for these women, part-time is all about choice. It's about having the opportunity to be involved in their communities, their families, and their children's schools, while keeping a foothold in their work. Says Mary, a journalist who uses part of her time outside work to be a room mother at her children's school: "I didn't have children so that we both could work full-time."

The Top 10 Industries Employing Women in Part-Time Jobs (1999)

- Eating and drinking places
- Elementary and secondary schools
- Hospitals
- Department stores
- Grocery stores
- Colleges and universities
- Private household services
- Nursing and personal care
- Child day care
- Health services (miscellaneous)

Who Gets It

There are two types of jobs that are part-time: those that are designed to be part-time and those that are not. Many of the jobs that are designed to be part-time are in industries that are often the lowest paying and the lowest skilled. In fact, half of all women who work part-time do so in just 10 out of 236 possible industries, and those industries have an average hourly wage of $8.26 to $20 less than the median wage of all workers.[4]

But then there's also the type of job that traditionally is full-time but somebody has managed to negotiate it to be part-time. The challenge is that many suggest that some of these jobs just don't lend themselves to part-time work. Among them are jobs in finance, sales, and customer service that require continual client contact. "Our experience is that anything where you need continual contact with a client does not work," says Kathleen Shelby of FlexTime Solutions. Isadora, the woman who runs a telecommuting public relations company, feels the same. Her company does not hire part-time workers as a general rule. "It doesn't work for most positions in our field," she says. The head of human resources of a marketing firm told me the same.

But to every rule there's an exception. In my research, I found part-time workers in all three of those fields. Likewise, some mothers told me that working part-time in a job that demanded strict deadlines also was not advisable. Yet again, I saw women arrange their part-time work to support strict deadlines by working for concentrated periods of time doing "project work." Yes clearly some jobs—particularly those that demand continual client contact or strict deadlines—will be harder to finesse into part-time. But given the right skills set and employer, that task is not impossible.

Is Part-Time Right for You?

In considering whether part-time is right for you, first look at your parenting needs and expectations. Do you feel you need or want time with your children that a full-time schedule can't support? Are 40 hours or more at the office too much? Do you feel you'll be able to sustain or support a closer relationship with your child if you work less?

Then consider your financial needs. Part-time no doubt bears an impact here, potentially above and beyond the proportionate decrease in time. For while it's hard to say exactly how much you will lose by going part-time, compensation per hour is lower in part-time than in full-time—even when jobs are from the same establishment and occupation.[5] In fact, one study showed that women who work part-time who have the same levels of education and experience and who have comparable family structures earn, on average, 20% less than their full-time counterparts.[6]

If you don't have to realize your full earning potential, that cut in pay may be just fine with you. If you get financial support through a spouse, ex, or partner, that adequately covers your family's costs or

if your skills are so valued that even part-time work pays the bills—
okay. But if your financial needs require that you pull in the maxi-
mum amount you can earn, part-time simply may not work for you.
That's what happened to Helen who has two children and worked
full-time as a director of client services at an Internet services firm.
She negotiated part-time work only to find that "I didn't make
enough money to support any of the amenities I need to work at
all," such as day care.

If you go part-time, your access to benefits may suffer as well.
One study shows that women who work part-time are 88% less likely
to receive health insurance or benefits.[7] Another shows that nearly
one fourth of workers employed part-time have no health insurance
at all,[8] and those who do get benefits tend to get lower benefits per
hour.[9] But not every part-timer goes without benefits. (Ahhh, so
that's what Starbucks is talking about.) Far from it. Nearly three
fourths of companies surveyed in one study offered part-timers
health and dental coverage.[10] It's often a matter of where you work.

Also, realize as you think about part-time work that job security
can be less certain[11] and career advancement, at a minimum, may be
sidelined for a time, as part-timers can be perceived as less committed to their employer and less deserving of good assignments and
promotions than their full-time counterparts. "You don't advance
your career this way. You just maintain it," says Marina of her position as a part-time management consultant in New Jersey. "It
somewhat slows down my career path," says Beatrice, a vice president for an electronic brokerage firm in Massachusetts, who works
four days a week. "If you're a manager and you go part-time, you
give up a lot in terms of advancement," says Charlotte, who worked
at a corporation as a marketing professional for 20 years. So, ask
yourself: Can you handle a plateau in your earnings for as long as
you work part-time?

Ask yourself too, from a professional perspective, if you feel it
necessary to advance quickly. As you consider that question, take

into account that part-time does not mean giving up on your career. It may slow your career, but probably won't derail it. A recent study by Catalyst, a nonprofit group for the advancement of women, tracked 24 senior-level women who used flexible work arrangements more than a decade ago and found more than half earned promotions over the past 10 years. Most of these women, the report says, credit the availability of part-time work schedules during critical child-rearing years as the key to maintaining career momentum. Most, too, still worked for the same company at which they had initiated flexible work arrangements earlier, averaging some 18 years in their organizations on the whole.[12] The other message here: loyalty pays.

Also think about your self-management skills. If the job you seek fits a full-time load better than a part-time one, the number of responsibilities can be difficult to complete in the hours you are *meant* to work. In fact, when Catalyst studied 2,000 managers they found that one barrier to successful implementation of part-time work arrangements was exactly that. More than half of participants reported that their workload did not change after reducing their working time (and salary). And 10% reported an *increase* in workload after reducing their working time.[13] "The challenge," says Beatrice, "is that you're working four days a week and pay is reduced by 20%, but the workload is not necessarily reduced. My four days are very busy." Agrees another woman who changed her job as an account manager back from part-time to full-time: "If you're part-time you've got to hurry up and do everything you've got to do." That workload can then extend into personal time as well, making it difficult for you to ever truly get away from your work. "Fridays are never completely 'off' as I check into the office three to five times a day and wear an e-mail pager constantly," says Barbara, an equity salesperson in Illinois.

So look at your self-management skills. Are you good at compartmentalizing? Are you organized? Are you structured? Can you say no? If you can't, learn. If not, you may find that engaging with your children, enjoying them, sustaining that relationship, which part-time is meant to support, simply does not work because you can never mentally get away from your work.

Of course, not all part-time work will require you to be on constant call or to cram a full week's work into a part-time week. In fact, if you set up your part-time work correctly, defining your responsibilities in a way that truly constitutes part-time work, you can avoid that crunch to some extent. Also, you may take on a part-time job that is already designed to be part-time and so does not have the same potential to creep into your personal life. However, remember that many of these jobs are lower paid.

Your work-content skills will also bear an impact on how well you can manage your part-time work. Are you going into a part-time job for which you are qualified, perhaps even overqualified, so that you don't have to chase your tail through the day? If that's the case and you don't end up getting the professional stimulation you like, how can you set up your life so that you meet the needs of that part of yourself in other ways? What interests can you pursue?

If your work-content skills don't match the job, are your transferable skills strong enough to enable you to transition smoothly enough so that you don't have to continually work overtime to feel you've got the job under control? Bear in mind, too, that a strong skills set will provide your prospective or current employer with a convincing case that you can get the job done well. "I wouldn't have gotten this job if I didn't have a proven track record," says Kylie, public relations executive from New Orleans who pioneered part-time work at her organization. Her sentiments echo those I heard over and over again among part-time professionals and managers. "I think the key is to have worked with the group for a long time and to have built trust and confidence," says Carolyn, a money manager from Connecticut.

Also be honest with yourself about why you're working. If, for

How to Make Part-Time Work

ESTABLISH YOUR LIMITS

If your potential job is already set up to be part-time, fine. If you're creating a position for which there was a full-time one or no job at all, be sure your work can be completed in the hours you work. That means sitting down with your supervisor and realistically assessing what's possible to complete in a part-time week and delegating tasks where you can, especially tasks to which you add little value. It may mean saying no to tasks and responsibilities that you know you could do well. It may mean, noted Kathleen Shelby earlier in this part of the book, that you "sacrifice some of your skills set." It may mean training others to do tasks you can't. Remember, you're choosing part-time to work less, not to work more without pay.

UNDERPROMISE AND OVERDELIVER

Remember Samantha's words: "Underpromise and overdeliver." This means once you're in that job, "don't be afraid to say no and set limits," as one mother in strategic planning and investment management says. Yes, you can overdeliver, but don't overpromise. If you do, you'll set yourself up to fail—either by not delivering on what you promised or by working hours that are meant to be time off.

MANAGE YOURSELF

You may find it hard to work in such concentrated bursts. To some extent, you'll have to change the way you work, blocking out interruptions that you might tolerate when full-time. "I find it helpful to avoid personal tasks on workdays. I try to make my work as close to 100% productive as possible," says Annabelle, a consultant and mother to one from Rhode Island.

THINK TEAMWORK

"It thrives on constant communication and teamwork," says Shelby of part-time work. You must maintain that communication on and—to some extent—off the

job as well. Establish regular meetings and times when you're in the office to discuss work-related concerns. One woman in marketing established what she
calls "touch base" meetings so she and colleagues know what the others are
doing. "I rely on my partners to be available when I'm not there," she says. Establishing what happens when she's *not* there is as important as establishing
what happens when she *is* there.

COMMUNICATE

As with flexible scheduling, use e-mail, the company office planner, even your
office door, to be sure people know your schedule at all times. When you're not
available, set up your phone mail, assistant (if relevant), and e-mail to direct
people to someone who can help. When you're not there, be sure you are not
totally out of bounds. Many women, while clear with colleagues that they do not
work on some days (even scheduling fixed nonwork events on those days so
they *can't* work), still make great efforts to stay abreast of their messages. They
check phone and e-mail messages, sometimes four or five times a day, "So no
question goes unanswered for very long," as one marketing consultant from California puts it. And when you first implement your schedule, remind people of it.
"In the beginning, I'd have to gently remind people that I was going. I'd have
to say I'm leaving by 2:30," says Claudia, an advertising account executive
from Ohio. You also may have to remind colleagues even after your work
arrangement is well established.

BE VISIBLE

Realize that as you will be at work less, you have to work harder to make yourself seen among workers when you're there. "You have to make yourself visi-
ble," says one mother. That doesn't mean attending every meeting. In fact,
many mothers suggest attending too many meetings prohibits you from giving
the time you need to your job. (Be discerning there.) But do introduce yourself to
new colleagues. Attend social gatherings when you can. Don't make your office
a hole that you climb into to put your head down, get your work done, and
leave. Stay connected.

FIND AN ADVOCATE

Because you're not there all the time, you'll need people who are willing to step in to back you up. When your status is called into question, you want people to say that your contributions are worth whatever inconveniences your arrangement creates. You'll need a supporter, someone who really values your work. That's why you're better off if you've worked in the organization full-time first and have done good work. If you don't have that support when starting your arrangement, work hard to establish it.

ESTABLISH YOUR COMPETITIVE SET

Minimize colleague resentment and foster support by defining yourself as a part-time employee who performs. Find where you can add value—even on part-time terms—and add it. That may be through servicing clients that want *you* even if on altered terms, as Kylie found. Or it may be, as Samantha found, through positioning yourself as reducing another's workload. "Anything I get done is something off your plate," she suggests. "I make sure my competitive set is not a five-day-a-week office worker," she says. Then be sure that employees are aware of the value you bring. To do that effectively, you will occasionally have to respond to jibes about your part-time status (directly and good-naturedly is best). You will have to point out your achievements and participate in performance reviews. You will need them to understand that you are paid in a manner proportionate to your contribution. "It may be impossible to avoid some level of resentment, so the key is to have the benefit of your input outweigh the negatives affected by the flexibility," says Cloe. Make sure that benefit is known.

REVIEW AND ASSESS

Once you have your arrangement in place, don't forget to regularly review and assess it. Set up regular reviews with your supervisor. If your arrangement is new to the company, set these more frequently at first—perhaps after the first two months—less frequently once the arrangement has been in place for a while. Be willing to discuss changing or altering your approach if you or your employer feels that business needs are not being met.

example, you look back at your needs and see that social stimulation, a chance to get out of the house, and an opportunity to earn a modest income of your own are professional values you expect your work to meet, then perhaps you don't want a high-pressure job.

Consider Job-Sharing

One way to deal with job demands that may not be suitable to traditional part-time work is to set up a job-sharing arrangement, an arrangement often touted as ideal for professional and management positions that need full-time coverage. It also may suit you if you want to work part-time but want to continue advancing your career; mothers say that job-sharing can bear less of a negative impact there.

Yet for all the sense it seems to make, job sharing—by which two people share a full-time job—is still relatively rare. In one recent study, some 40% of employers offered job sharing and yet only 3% of employees took advantage of it.[14] Job-sharing is more commonly offered among larger companies than small,[15] but even among larger companies of 500 or more, a utilization rate of 3% is certainly quite small.

Why is job-sharing not taken advantage of more often? Well, for one thing it requires putting a lot of pieces in the right place. First, the employer and supervisor have to support the idea. Convincing them can be a battle if the company budgets for employees by counting heads rather than full-time equivalents. It is a challenge, by the way, that any part-time worker who wants full-time benefits will face if her employer bases benefits on the number of heads because two employees in the place of one mean added costs, something from which some managers will shy away. But that is surmountable. As a job-sharer, you may be able to allow one of the partners to take full benefits if one gets benefits through a spouse. Pro-rating benefits also is an option for some.

Once more, as few take advantage of job-sharing—fewer, by the way, than those who take advantage of traditional part-time work—there's a lot of education to be done. The manager and employer may wonder if it really can work if so few people opt to pursue it at all. Likewise, managing one job between two people has inherent challenges. Can two people effectively manage and execute one job? Will it be confusing to clients, colleagues, and others who deal with job sharers? Will continuity be lost? What happens if the situation doesn't work out or work suffers as a result? Will setting up the arrangement require too much time from an already overworked manager? All of these questions may be addressed if the arrangement is set up appropriately (see the box How to Make Job-Sharing Work), but think first about whether job-sharing could work for you.

Is It Right for You?

To assess whether job-sharing is appropriate for you, begin by using the same criteria you used in assessing your suitability for part-time work as a whole. Can you still meet your financial needs given the decrease in pay and potential lack of benefits? Are your work-content skills strong and relevant enough for you to take on the position seamlessly? If not, do you have transferable skills that are so strong that you may even be perceived as overqualified for the job and may be able to dedicate the extra time initially, if necessary, to learn the work-content skills you need?

Then look at the job you want to do. Does it qualify as professional or managerial? Does it make more sense, in that job, to make it a job-share than simply to delegate tasks that you can't get done on a part-time basis? As far as your own professional needs are concerned, will you be more satisfied if you are able to maintain some potential for advancement, as you may be able to do in a job-sharing arrangement? Will it meet the professional needs you set out?

How to Make Job-Sharing Work

BE SURE YOU BOTH HAVE THE RIGHT SKILLS

Employees must have the right attributes to make it work. Among those, employers and job-sharers say, are not only work-content and transferable skills that fit the job but an ability to communicate well and strong organizational skills. Writing everything down and systematically organizing are key. "It creates tremendous resentment if you walk into the office and [the job-sharing arrangement] creates more work," says Claire, the woman featured in the introduction of this book. If your strengths complement one another (as in a good marriage, job sharers often say), your job-sharing team may bring more to the job than a single person could, but core skills must be strong. Make sure your communication styles mesh as well. To find that person look within the company or draw on your professional network. Find someone who complements your skills and has similar objectives and goals toward work. "Similar job experiences and backgrounds but a little bit different from each other," is how one job-sharing mother puts it. Realize, as Claire notes, "that person becomes a life partner" of sorts. Think *we* not *I* when it comes to your work.

WORK OUT HOW YOU WILL DIVIDE THE WORK

Experts suggest you work out the details of how you're going to split your job share before you approach your boss. How will you break down the work-week, cover sick days, child illnesses and emergencies, and vacation days? Schedule coverage so that there are few times when both are absent. Many job sharers choose to break the week in half, overlapping for an hour or so on Wednesday to connect. Also look at the job and its tasks and responsibilities. Based on your respective experience, strengths, and preferences determine who should handle which job responsibilities and clients.

COME UP WITH YOUR COMMUNICATION PLAN

How will you contact one another when issues arise? How often will you check in with one another? What will you do if issues arise that you can't handle? And how will you maintain continuity with one another as well as your colleagues, bosses, and clients? Will you leave notes for one another each day in a file? Will you e-mail one another, leave voice mail, schedule catch-up meetings for Wednesdays? Will you establish a job-sharing binder to store all notes and all of the day's work for both partners' review? Will you take copies home with you of important documents so you are informed if your partner calls? One job-sharer told me she has found it useful to keep a running log of all projects, details, and FYIs, and to make regular use of e-mail. After her time off, she dials into that log and those e-mails before she goes into the office the next day.

DETERMINE YOUR TERMS

Work out how you might break down salary and benefits given existing company policy on part-time work. Does one of you get benefits through a spouse or is pro-rating benefits a possibility at your employer? If the company offers full-time benefits to part-time staff, be prepared to justify the costs.

ENLIST AND MAINTAIN COMPANY SUPPORT

Get colleagues on board by showing how the arrangement works. Maintain consistency with work projects. Finish work on time. Return phone calls in a timely manner. Be responsive. "It also definitely works to your advantage if your bosses support your job share and not just accept it because it is in place. Their support helps support your success. Without it, you could be the best team ever, but people will always complain about something," says Cassandra.

DON'T BE AFRAID TO SELF-PROMOTE

Take advantages of opportunities to show that you're getting the job done and doing it well. If you receive backhanded remarks, point out your value. If you hear, "Sorry, I forgot you, but I never see you." Answer, "You can see one of us working hard every day to make sure your presentation goes well." If you don't have the courage to reply, to stand up for yourself, find it. Don't let people lose sight of your team's value.

REVIEW AND ASSESS

Once you have your job-sharing arrangement in place, don't forget to regularly review and assess it. Set up regular reviews with your supervisor and your job-sharing partner. Set these more frequently at first—perhaps after the first two months—less frequently once the arrangement has been in place for a while. Be willing to discuss changing or altering your approach if you or your employer feels that business needs are not being met.

If the answers to those questions are yes, consider your self-management skills. Do you store checklists in your head or do you write things down? Can you see yourself being organized enough to effectively share a role? Are you a good enough communicator to function with a partner as if you had two heads? Do you have some potential partners in mind?

Based on what you've read, if you think part-time work or job-sharing is what you seek, check the item on your bookmark.

Real Mother Recap

Well, that about covers part-time work, including traditional part-time and job-sharing arrangements. To sum up, part-time work usually means sacrificing pay and sometimes benefits in part or in whole. If part-time arrangements are common at a particular employer or industry, securing and managing it will be easier. If you are a professional or manager in an industry or business for which part-time arrangements are rare, you have a harder task and are better off if you are currently employed there. If part-time is not viable, you may consider job-sharing instead. If you do job-share, however, remember organization and management skills are key.

If you need more information: For specific information on part-time work, the U.S. Office of Personnel Management has a guide to part-time employment and job-sharing at www.opm.gov/workfam/pt-employ/pt01.htm. Visit www.sharegoals.com, which contains helpful information on job-sharing.

13

Being Your Own Boss

I put everything into it. When it's your own business, you learn how much you have to put into it.

—TERESA

TERESA

The life of military spouses is not easy. Because they move often—rarely in one location for more than two or three years at a time—many find it hard to get good jobs, even harder to advance or build careers. If they decide they can meet their and their family's needs by stepping out of the workforce, fine. But for some, the need or desire to work is more pressing.

Teresa, 39 years old, is one such woman. Like many military spouses, she lived a peripatetic life, both abroad and in the United States. Living out of the country with small children, she didn't consider working an option then. "I got very wrapped up in being a mother to my babies," she says. But once her children grew a little, she began to ask herself, "Now what do I do?" She decided she wanted a business she and her husband, Scott, could run after he retired from the army and that, until then, could go wherever Scott was stationed. She investigated a few franchise op-portunities but opted to start something on her own instead.

During their family's six-year stay in Europe, Teresa and her husband had visited a town in Poland known for its traditional folk art ceramics. She had loved the wares and purchased some to take home. Then, one day as she sat thinking about what business she could run, selling Polish pottery sprang to mind.

For the next year and a half, Teresa researched. She checked out library books on how to build a business, how to market, and did a lot of Internet research. She contacted a Dutch acquain-tance in the import/export business to discuss the intricacies of buying, packing, and shipping. She found a person who spoke Pol-ish to help her communicate with factory management. And then, when she returned to Melbourne, Florida, she contacted the Small Business Administration's Service Corp (SCORE) for help on starting up a small business. Did she have any doubts she could do it? Of course. "I kept saying to myself, other people can do this. I can do this," she says.

In October 1999, Teresa launched her company, www.polishpottery.com. In just two years, she managed the business to gross over $300,000 and secured distribution in excess of 200 stores. She set up distribution networks through a group of at-home workers (most of them in the military) and a Web site and worked with nonprofit organizations for fund-raising projects. She even won a small business award of the year through her local SCORE chapter.

But for Teresa, the business is a success for more than the money it generates or its portability. He business meshes with what she wants out of family life. "If you can have a [home] business that can be profitable, the benefits are so much better for the kids." Moreover, she believes what has helped make her business a success are her experiences and skills as a mother—"the skills I used as a Daisy leader, room leader, the derivatives of being a mother, like

> ## Portable Business for Military Spouses
>
> To help meet the growing need for portable businesses, the Small Business Administration (SBA) and the Department of Defense have funded a two-year pilot program to provide entrepreneurial training to military spouses to help them develop businesses that can easily move with their families. For more information, visit: www.onlinewbc.gov/docs/military_content/index.html.

coordinating people." Yes, hours can be long, she says, estimating that she works on average 12 hours a day, sometimes late into the night. But she is still able to get up with her children, take them to school, and even enlist their support to do tasks like putting stamps on envelopes. "This is my kind of business," she says.

In case you've missed it, the number of women who are self-employed (among them small business owners, freelancers, contractors, consultants, even some on-call and temporary workers) is one the rise. In 2000, women represented some 38% of the self-employed.[1] Women-owned businesses are now increasing at twice the rate of all firms. In fact, privately-held, women-owned firms in the United States account for some 28% of all privately-held firms in the country.[2] No small potatoes.

Why are they doing it? The reasons are multifold. The most common reason, according to one study of 800 business owners, is that—lo and behold—these women have good ideas! That shouldn't surprise you. You're full of them, right? The second is that these women are frustrated with their current work environments because they want more flexibility from their work,[3] something that mother after mother says she needs to tend to the demands that parenting brings.

The Benefits to Being Self-Employed

Being your own boss can bring many advantages to mothers trying to manage work and home. The first is flexibility, particularly if the business is a one-woman show, as the majority of women-owned firms are.[4] Why particularly one-woman shows? Well, if you run out of the office to pick up your children, no one will know if no one is *in* that office. Yes, like Teresa you may work late into the night some days, but you also may be able to pop out to put the kids on the bus. "It is the only way to work," says one mother from Oklahoma.

Being your own boss also can be extremely empowering. You control your hours, your input, and the creative and professional direction of your career. You have an ownership of your work that many women find very rewarding in itself.[5] As Teresa pointed out at the beginning of this chapter, "I never knew I had so much to put in." No boss can thwart your advancement by telling you that your idea won't work or that your home commitments leave her in doubt of your commitment to your work. That empowerment not only benefits you but also benefits your relationship with your kids. Studies have shown that a job environment that is rewarding, challenging, and thought to be autonomous is more likely to help mothers—particularly mothers with young children—feel capable and able to cope with the demands of family life.[6] A job that you create and control can be just that.

But be warned, making that choice also carries some serious risks. Those long hours may eventually get you down, even if you are putting in a lot of them when the kids are asleep. The lack of security may leave you feeling anxious. The lack of support may leave you feeling alone. And if the job does leave you stressed—emotionally, professionally, or financially—it may preclude you from giving your parent-child relationship what it needs. That's not to mention the financial liability of starting a business of your own, a liability that if it

Nancy's Advice for Entrepreneurial Mothers*

Mothers often feel stretched in too many directions, particularly if they work outside the home. Being the mother of twin girls (9 months old when I started my first business and 11 years old when I started my second) and an entrepreneur, I often get asked about how I managed to start my businesses and raise children at the same time. That's a huge question, and I've tried to distill my advice into a few basic points. Every mother who's thinking of starting a business needs to think about these things.

In many ways, starting a business is just like having a child: It completely changes your life; it brings out both the best and the worst in you; it takes more time, money, creativity, and energy than you could ever imagine beforehand; it goes through stages and keeps you guessing; it stirs deep pride in you at unexpected moments; it gradually takes on its own life and identity, separate from you; it gives back energy and enriches your life in immeasurable ways.

• Be sure you are passionate about your business—if not, it's hard to get through the rocky times. It's easier (but not crucial) if your partner is supportive and excited about your business. You're going to need him or her (or someone else) to do more than 50% of the child and household duties at times.

• Seek advice from the Small Business Development Center near you (check out www.sba.gov/sbdc). That's where I learned to analyze and use financial statements and projections and got connected to other small business owners, who are an invaluable sounding board.

• Set clear financial goals that include paying yourself and other workers and growing the business's revenues.

• Keep expenses and overhead (rent, equipment, optional travel, fancy furnishings) as low as possible—they erode your bottom line and should be delayed when cash is tight.

• If you plan to co-own the business with a friend or acquaintance, spend the time and money to get some business counseling together before getting into any legally binding situation. You need to be sure you're on the same wavelength with your expectations, and a skilled facilitator can provide crucial objective feedback. Particularly if it's a friend, it can be hard to see problems that may be looming based on different expectations.

• If possible, work for a while in the type of business you want to start. This will give you invaluable knowledge and perspective when getting started.

• Add fun in wherever you can. Being serious is my personality, and so I have to remind myself that goofing off is important to keep my balance emotionally and healthwise.

• Involve your kids in the business as much as they want. It can be a great way to spend time together, and it gives them a head start if they ever decide to start their own business.

• If you run the business from your home, try to establish healthy boundaries between work and free time. But face it, a start-up business is not a nine to five proposition, and you will often be answering e-mails, reviewing financials, and hatching marketing plans while the rest of your family is asleep. At the same time, entrepreneurial types can also be workaholics (I plead guilty), and family is the ideal antidote to workaholism. A child who demands that you pay attention to her can yank you away from the computer and keep your perspective real.

Starting my own business was the most exciting, rewarding, and frustrating thing I've ever done—besides raising my daughters. I think it will be for you, too.

*Nancy Gruver is founder and CEO of New Moon Publishing, creator of the award-winning *New Moon: The Magazine for Girls and Their Dreams* (www.newmoon.org).

Temporary Workers

Some argue that temporary work can be a family-friendly arrangement. You may be one of them. Temporary work allows you to work for self-selected periods of time. You make no long-term commitment to an employer, providing some flexibility in how you decide to direct your career long-term and to try out different employers and jobs. You get an opportunity to exercise some skills and keep your foot in the market without committing yourself long term. You also may get the opportunity to prove yourself and then convert your position into full-time (though it's difficult to find research to support that conclusion).* That's all well and good, but what you also have to realize is that workers in these arrangements are more likely to earn lower wages, have less job security, and have fewer benefits. Many in those positions also would rather work on standard terms.† So before you choose this route, make sure it's right for you.

*Despite temp industry assertions that temp work is a "bridge to permanent employment," federal and industry survey data indicate otherwise. Among those studies supporting that view: Susan N. Houseman's "New Institute Survey on Flexible Staffing Arrangements" Employment Research (Upjohn Institute for Employment Research, Spring 1997).
†Ken Hudson, No Shortage of "Nonstandard" Jobs [EPI Briefing Paper] (Washington, DC: Economic Policy Institute, 1999). Also see Susan N. Houseman, Flexible Staffing Arrangements [Executive Summary] (Washington, DC: U.S. Department of Labor. 1999).

were to go wrong could leave you not only without a job and income but without savings as well.

Financial Needs

So how do you even start to assess whether being your own boss is right for you? Well, first do what you did at the start of this book:

Identify your financial needs. Whether you're starting your own small business or becoming an independent contractor, consultant or freelancer ("free agent" in New Economy parlance), you are taking on a financial risk. Sit down with your spouse or partner, accountant, and/or financial planner and determine how much you need to earn from your business and whether that's viable given what you seek to do. Make sure what you can charge or earn covers living expenses and the cost of any insurance or savings that you need to meet.

What your self-employed arrangement provides financially—at least in the short term—could be significantly less. It may be a while, for example, before you see an income, even if potentially you could make more down the line. As one copy writer (whose husband was a student) told me when her company folded and she was forced to go freelance: "You can spend a lot of time waiting for those checks to come in even after you've done the work." Second, unless you and your family qualify for benefits through a spouse, health insurance, life insurance, and other typically employer-sponsored benefits will be more expensive. And third, your business may not last. As you probably know, the failure rates of new businesses are very high. According to the Small Business Administration, one third of businesses fail within the first two years, about one half close within four years, and about three fifths close within six.[7] In other words, if you don't like taking on risk, you may want to think twice when it comes to setting up your own shop.

If you're a woman, you've got a better chance of making that business work. Nearly three quarters of women-owned firms in business overall in 1991 were still in business three years later, compared to two thirds of all U.S. firms.[8] (One reason may be that women business owners are more likely to run a one-woman show. Thus set-up costs are lower, risks are smaller, and "failure" is less succinct.)

But if you are starting a small business, bear in mind that the amount of time planning a new business is said to be directly related to its success. So if you are going beyond becoming a free agent, be sure you have a thorough business plan and all that it entails. Know projected costs, funding sources, your competition, the marketplace, where to go for support and advice, and how to exit should the business fail. And that's just the start. There are countless books and support networks out there for budding entrepreneurs. SCORE and the SBA (they even have a Women's Business Center) are two places to start.

Also consider your parenting needs and the type of arrangement you are considering setting up. Are you planning on freelance or consultant projects that allow you time to meet your children's needs? Or are you planning to start a business in which the demands may be 24/7? What is realistic given your parenting needs and the schedule they demand? Is your work something you can do from home? Will it have tight deadlines? How much flexibility will you have? Will you be managing or a one-woman show? What kind of pressure will you face to make your work a success? Will that pressure preclude you from being able to engage with your children the way you want or need? Will you also be able to give the time to your partner that your relationship needs?

If you are starting a business for which you will be providing something other than your skills set (i.e., not simply freelancing), do you believe in and enjoy what you are doing? It's important to enjoy what you do no matter what your arrangement. But for better or worse, mothers sometimes sacrifice that enjoyment to some extent until their children are older, so that they can meet pressing financial or parenting concerns. But if you are starting your own business for which you will be devoting a significant amount of time and perhaps even financial resources, your outlook should be more long term. You most likely will work long hours, even if flexible ones, so you better enjoy what you do. "Find your passion," says Jessica, who runs a business that provides science programs for children. "Do what you love," agrees Jane who left her career as an investment banker to run a travel-consulting firm. So take a hard look at your interests, your professional values, and the skills you most enjoy. Make sure your business is where these intersect.

Look, too, at those self-management skills you identified in Step Two. Can you work independently? Are you self-disciplined? Are you self-confident and tenacious? Do you like to be in control? Are you able to make decisions? Are you innovative and creative? Are you optimistic? (When business is slow you'll need to be able to keep your spirits up.) Can you learn from your mistakes? Can you take initiative? If you're going to be self-employed—either building a business or acting as a Free Agent—you need to have "just answered yes" a lot.

If you want to become a free agent, draw on strong work-content skills that can be easily used in that capacity. These are skills you can use independently and include accounting, analysis, design, editing, researching, and writing. Consider using them on that basis with your current employer, at least at the start. Why? Because a current employer knows your skills, you'll cost less, and he can terminate you when he needs to—all of which can make a more compelling case for hiring you as a free agent. To supplement that work, source business through a network of people for whom you've done work before or who value what you can do. If, for example, you have accounting skills, approach a fellow nursery school board member for leads on accounting work because she's seen the great job you've done keeping the school's books. If you are starting your own business, be sure your transferable skills, if not your work-content skills, match up. If you are starting your own business and your work-content skills don't match up, invest some time in getting those skills up to scratch—by doing a stint at a related company, taking courses, or investing more time on the job, if it doesn't put your business at risk. If after you read the tips below you decide being your own boss is what you want, check that on your bookmark.

When You're Your Own Boss

BE PROFESSIONAL

Set up your business properly with a filing system, accurate books, a proper workspace (the dining room table doesn't qualify), and everything else that a successfully run business requires, from filing tax returns to keeping track of invoices to sorting mail. Also key are a business phone (your five-year-old acting as secretary doesn't cut it), e-mail system (automatic reply when relevant), fax, decent computer system with Internet access (preferably high speed), and whatever else is needed to create a professional communication system for your work. No one needs to know you're a mom working on her own or running a business where flexible hours reign. You're a professional. Start being one.

PERFORM

"They have to see the quality of my work first," says Tanya, a consultant and mother of three. For if your client sees that you can do a good job, that you can deliver, then your arrangement—even if it is a small business or a one-woman show—will not matter. Concentrate on that first. A strong performance will help you build a good reputation and even may secure you a reference for more work down the line. Don't grow your business at the cost of what you produce.

MANAGE YOUR TIME

Set up a schedule to your day to avoid slipping out of the office to unload the dishwasher. If you tend to lose yourself in e-mailing and personal phone calls, schedule those when you're least effective. Schedule commitments to your kids as well. Allow for the odd demand or emergency, but work from a basic schedule, and you'll get more done. "Organization is always a plus. If you have a little focus you can get so much more finished in a day. Prioritize," says Jessica, that mother of three who runs a science programs for kids.

STAY CONNECTED

Whether you're a free agent or building a business, your network is key. Don't isolate yourself in your office. If you are doing project work as a free agent, occasionally work out of a client's office, if viable. Schedule regular face-to-face meetings with clients, prospective clients, and contacts. Join professional associations, attend conferences, socialize and volunteer when you can. Stay abreast of the marketplace. "A wide social network is key," says Charlotte, an executive career coach in Missouri. "People who work like viruses do better. I'm always talking to the person next to me." Also maintain and update your skills set. Staying current is often harder work when working for yourself.

SELL

If you're hesitant to pick up the phone and make a cold call, *get over it!* You are running your own business, whether you are a free agent or small business owner. Yes, you may be selling skills, services, or a product, but you are *selling,* and you won't get the work unless you do just that. Advises Charlotte to women thinking of working on their own, "If they can't do sales, they should not do this."

BE ABLE TO WALK AWAY

Remember the importance of being able to connect with your children when you're with them. Don't let the stress of being your own boss preclude you from being able to turn off the computer, leave your office, and engage with your child when you've committed yourself. "You have to have the discipline to walk away at the end of the day." says Sarah, a self-employed marketing consultant from Mississippi. "I know when to leave it."

MAKE SURE YOUR FAMILY IS ON BOARD

Support from your family is essential. They can be cheerleaders when times are tough, extra hands when you need to get that last-minute mailing out, and sympathetic when you've got to unexpectedly work. "When I've had self-doubts, they've kept me going," says one small business owner from Utah. Also realize that your family can probably do more than you give them credit for. You don't have to do all the household jobs, for example. Work toward establishing an atmosphere at home where is everyone is eager to pitch in for the common good. Sharing tasks with a partner means sharing the power of running a home.

You're in this life together—as a family unit—and you all carry responsibilities to make it work.

REMEMBER CHILD CARE

Given your family's needs, you have to decide the child-care arrangement that works. Don't assume that running your own business gives you the opportunity to simultaneously care for your kids. Multitasking won't work here. Your children need your full attention and so does your business—separately. Don't expect to get away with giving half to each. Sure, if you've got a business that is child-related or for which you don't have direct interface with clients, there may be times they can help you with menial tasks. But it's your job, not theirs. If, given your prospective income, you find you have to simultaneously care for the children and the business, then running your own business is probably not right for you.

Real Mother Recap

Being your own boss is the final family-friendly job arrangement I address. If being your own boss appeals to you, be sure you are in a financial position to accommodate that arrangement, as the risks are higher, the job security lower, and the income in the short term potentially less (in the long term, you might make more). Just be sure you are equipped with the job skills, ideas, and self-management skills you need. Also be sure your family is on board. And don't forget about child care. Working for yourself does not mean you can simultaneously care for the kids. To thrive, work and children need you, full on, when you're there.

If you need more information: Many resources exist for you—too many to list here. You may want to start with the Small Business Association's Online Women's Business Center (www.onlinewbc.gov).

NOTES

Chapter 9

1. In 1989, Felice Schwartz, founder of the nonprofit group for the advancement of women called Catalyst, wrote an article in the *Harvard Business Review* suggesting that employers create policies to assist mothers in balancing career and family by giving them more flexibility and providing high-quality day care. She was derided for suggesting a "Mommy Track." See Felice N. Schwartz, "Management of Women and the New Facts of Life," *Harvard Business Review,* January 1, 1989.

2. One survey found that utilization rates at companies that offered the benefit were, on average, 33% for flextime; 16% for compressed workweeks; 9% for part-time; 8% for telecommuting; and 3% for job-sharing. Reported in William M. Mercer Inc. and Bright Horizons Family Solutions, *Survey Report: Work/Life Initiatives 2000* (2001).

Chapter 10

1. A total of 39.2% of female-headed households with children under 18 years old live in poverty, according to Table 1 in Bernadette D. Proctor, Joseph Dalaker, and the U.S. Census Bureau, *Poverty in the United States: 2001* [Current Population Reports P60–219] (Washington, DC: U.S. Government Printing Office, 2002).

2. Catalyst, The National Foundation for Women Business Owners (NFWBO), and The Committee of 200, *Paths to Entrepreneurship: New Directions for Women in Business* (sponsored by Salomon Smith Barney, 1998). Press release available at www.catalystwomen.org/press/release0224.html; accessed on: April 2, 2003.

3. Catalyst, *Flexible Work Arrangements: A Fact Sheet* (referenced study: Catalyst, *Flexible Work Arrangements II: Succeeding with Part-Time Options,* 1993). Available at www.catalystwomen.org/press_room/factsheets/factflex_work.htm; accessed on: April 2, 2003.

4. As found in survey of 1,057 companies with 100 or more employees. Ellen Galinsky and James T. Bondin, *The 1998 Business Work-Life Study: A Sourcebook* (New York: Families and Work Institute).

5. From the *Report on the American Workforce 1999,* by the U.S. Bureau of Labor Statistics, cited in "The Editor's Desk: Incidence of Flexible Work Schedules Increases," *Monthly Labor Review,* September 30, 1999.

6. Bureau of Census for the Bureau of Labor Statistics, *Workers on Flexible and Shift Schedules in 2001* (Washington, DC: U.S. Department of Labor).

7. Lonnie Golden, "Flexible Work Schedules: What Are We Trading Off to Get Them?" *Monthly Labor Review,* March 2001, p. 53.

8. From the May 1997 supplement to the Current Population Survey by the Bureau of Labor Statistics, cited in "The Editor's Desk: Executives Most Likely to Have Flexible Work Hours," *Monthly Labor Review,* July 26, 2000.

9. *Survey Report: Work/Life Initiatives 2000.*

10. Ibid.

11. These points were made by Golden, "Flexible Work Schedules."

12. Ibid.

Chapter 11

1. Department of Labor, *Telework and The New Workplace of the 21st Century—Executive Summary* (Washington, DC: U.S. Department of Labor). Based on a national symposium at Xavier University, New Orleans, October 16, 2000. Available at: www.dol.gov/asp/telework/execsum.htm; accessed on: April 2, 2003.

2. Donald D. Davis and Karen A. Polonko, "Telework in the United States: Telework America Survey 2001" (Old Dominion University, Norfolk, Virginia, October 2001).

3. Department of Labor, *Telework and The New Workplace of the 21st Century—Executive Summary* (Washington, DC: U.S. Department

of Labor). Based on a national symposium at Xavier University, New Orleans, October 16, 2000. Available at: www.dol/gov/asp/telework/execsum.htm; accessed on: April 2, 2003.

4. Bureau of Labor Statistics, *Work at Home 2001*. Based on the May 2001 Current Population Survey.

5. Susan Seitel, "Update on Telecommuting" (Minnetonka, MN: Work & Family Connection, 2001).

6. *Telework and The New Workplace of the 21st Century.*

7. William M. Mercer Inc. and Bright Horizons Family Solutions, *Survey Report: Work/Life Initiatives 2000* (2001).

8. *Work at Home 2001.*

9. *Telework and The New Workplace of the 21st Century.*

Chapter 12

1. Vivien Corwin, Thomas B. Lawrence and Peter J. Frost, "Five Strategies of Successful Part-time Work," *Harvard Business Review,* July–August 2001, p. 122. The authors write: "nearly 10% of the professional workforce now works part-time." The Bureau of Labor Statistics for 2001 show that just over 18% of those under the classification of "managerial and professional specialty" work 1 to 34 hours. Bureau of Census for the Bureau of Labor Statistics, Current Population Survey, 2001 (Washington, DC: U.S. Department of Labor, 2001). Table #23, "Persons at work in nonfarm occupations by sex and usual full- or part-time status"). Available at: www.bls.gov/cps/cpsaat21.pdf; accessed on: April 2, 2003.

2. Roberta M. Spalter-Roth, Arne L. Kalleberg, Edith Rasel, Naomi Cassirer, Barbara F. Reskin, Ken Hudson, David Webster, Eileen Appelbaum, Betty L. Dooley, *Managing Work and Family: Nonstandard Work Arrangements among Managers and Professionals* (Washington DC: Economic Policy Institute, 1997).

3. Bureau of Census for the Bureau of Labor Statistics, "Earnings of part-timers," *Monthly Labor Review,* July 02, 2003. Available at:

www.bls.gov/opub/ted/2002/jul/wk1/art02.htm; accessed on: April 2, 2003.

4. As found in survey of 1,057 companies with 100 or more employees and cited in the Executive Summary of Ellen Galinsky and James T. Bondin, *The 1998 Business Work-Life Study: A Sourcebook* (New York: Families and Work Institute, 1988).

5. From the *Report on the American Workforce 1999*, by the U.S. Bureau of Labor Statistics, cited in "The Editor's Desk: Incidence of Flexible Work Schedules Increases," *Monthly Labor Review,* September 30, 1999. Available at www.bls.gov/opub/ted/1999/sept/wk5/art04.htm; accessed on: April 2, 2003.

6. Bureau of Census for the Bureau of Labor Statistics, *Workers on Flexible Shift Schedules in 2001* (Washington, DC: U.S. Department of Labor, 2002).

7. Ibid.

8. From the May 1997 supplement to the Current Population Survey by the Bureau of Labor Statistics, cited in "The Editor's Desk: Executives Most Likely to Have Flexible Work Hours," *Monthly Labor Review,* July 26, 2000. Available at: www.bls.gov/opub/ted/2000/jul/wk4/art03.htm; accessed on: April 2, 2003.

9. William M. Mercer Inc. and Bright Horizons Family Solutions, *Survey Report: Work/Life Initiatives 2000* (2001).

10. A survey of 350 large U.S. companies looked at policies for those working at least 30 hours per week, compared them to 1995, and found that more than three fourths of companies offer part-timers health and dental coverage. Hewitt Associates, *United States Salaried Work/Life Benefits,* 1999 (Lincolnshire, IL: Hewitt Associates, LLC 2000).

11. Susan Housemant and Anne E. Polinke, *The Implications of Flexible Staffing Arrangement for Job Security* (Washington, DC: Bureau of Labor Statistics, 1998).

12. Catalyst, *Flexible Work Arrangements III: A Ten-Year Retrospective of Part-Time Arrangements for Managers and Professionals* (2000).

Press release available at: www.catalystwomen.org/press_room/ press_releases/flex_work_three.htm; accessed on: April 2, 2003.

13. Harriet B. Presser, "Nonstandard Work Schedules and Marital Instability," *Journal of Marriage and Family:* vol 62, no. 1, 2000. 93–110.

14. William M. Mercer Inc. and Bright Horizons Family Solutions, *Survey Report: Work/Life Initiatives 2000* (2001).

15. Society of Human Resource Management Survey Program, *2002 Benefits Survey* (Alexandria, VA: SHRM, 2002).

Chapter 13

1. Dr. Ying Lowrey, *Women in Business, 2001* (Washington, DC: U.S. Small Business Administration Office of Advocacy, 2001).

2. Between 1997 and 2002, the number of women-owned firms increased at twice the rate of all firms (14% vs. 7%), employment grew at 1.5 times the rate (30% vs. 18%), and revenues increased at the same rate. Center for Women's Business Research, *Women-Owned Businesses in the United States, 2002: A Fact Sheet* (underwritten by Wells Fargo Bank, 2001). Available at: www.nfwbo.org/USStateFacts/ US.pdf; accessed on: March 14, 2003.

3. Catalyst, The National Foundation for Women Business Owners (NFWBO), and The Committee of 200, *Paths to Entrepreneurship: New Directions for Women in Business.* (sponsored by Salomon Smith Barney 1998). Press release available at: www.catalystwomen.org/ press/release0224.html; accessed on: April 2, 2003.

4. In 1997, the vast majority of women-owned firms (4.6 million, or 85%) were sole proprietorships, unincorporated businesses owned by individuals. U.S. Census Bureau, *1997 Economic Census Surveys of Minority- and Women-Owned Businesses* (Washington, DC: Economics and Statistics Administration, Bureau of the Census, 2001). Available at: www.census.gov/Press-Release/www/2001/cb01-61. html; accessed on: April 3, 2002.

5. Aquent and Penn Schoen & Berland, *1099 Index* (Boston, MA: Aquent, 2001). Job placement agency Aquent commissioned na-

tional polling firm Penn Schoen & Berland to survey 800 "independent professionals" (self-employed, temporary, contract, freelance, or on-call workers) and found that among the 49% of women in the poll, 87% percent preferred working independently versus working in a traditional job; 69% were very satisfied with their jobs versus 53% of W-2 women; 54% said their work provides a good work–life balance versus 42% of W-2 women.

6. Ellen Galinsky and James T. Bond, *Helping Families with Young Children Navigate Work and Family Life* (New York, Families and Work Institute).

7. Small Business Association's Office of Advocacy study of businesses over 1989–1992.

8. Office of Women's Business Ownership, *Statistics on Women's Business Ownership,* June 1996 (Washington DC: U.S. Small Business Administration, 1996). Available at: www.sba.gov/gopher/Business-Development/Womens-Business-Ownership/stats.txt; accessed on: April 2, 2003.

STEP FOUR

Get Family-Friendly Work

14

Plan Your Search

Whatever you do in your life, you know people. Just let them know what you need.

—VERONICA

VERONICA

"The biggest thing I feared is that I didn't feel ready to go back to work."

Those were the sentiments of Veronica, a 40-year-old mother of four whose husband had just passed away. After 15 years out of the workforce, how was she going to do it? She had been a buyer in a department store before the birth of her first child, but for a woman who needed accessibility to home, retail at that level was not a viable profession. She was at a loss. She turned to her immediate network for help.

"I went around and talked to a lot of people," she recalls. "I talked to a husband of a dear friend. Maybe I could be a receptionist, I thought. But I didn't even have secretarial skills."

Meanwhile, her cousin's wife was a teacher who encouraged her to go into teaching. She didn't want to become a teacher at first, but given the demands of four children, aged 14 to 6, she recognized that she needed a paying job that allowed her to be home after school and on holidays. "It was tough," she says. She contacted the State of Pennsylvania, where she lived, and discovered that she could get a temporary teaching credential. It came quickly and she became a kindergarten substitute. "It wasn't right. I couldn't control the kids."

She then started taking classes to teach English and ran into an old acquaintance, a superintendent at a nearby school. "I went to him and said 'I'm not a teacher and I have four children I have to support.'" He told her of an opening in grade school for fourth-grade English. He took a chance on her. "I came to love it," she says.

Her teaching career went through several stages after that. She taught marketing to high school students—an idea that she got through an acquaintance she saw at a hairdressing salon. She got her master's degree; moved to California with a few contacts in hand, thanks to some people she had come to know in Philadelphia; trained in career development; and started teaching at the University of California at San Diego (UCSD) in a certificate program. She even managed a federal grant for single parents and displaced homemakers for eight years.

Now, she's a part-time teacher at UCSD, president of a nonprofit that centers on work–life issues, and sole proprietor of a career counseling practice. To what does she attribute her success? Four supportive children—the oldest of whom took on the brunt of responsibility at home, her church, and an almost intuitive sense of what is needed to get a job.

"I was really smart in how I connected to people," she recalls. "Whatever you do in your life, you know people. Just let them know what you need." Synchronicity is a word she likes. "If you put your antenna out and you're listening and alert, you'll find opportunity. You will find links through acquaintances," she says,

pointing to what some call the strength of weak ties. "You have to reach out."

You should have a fair idea of possible arrangements that support your needs and utilize your strengths. Now, it's time to find the right job. To do that, you need a strategy. You need to establish where to start your search for family-friendly work and who can facilitate that.

This chapter will help you understand what that strategy requires. As you pursue it, your network will be key. Your network can provide leads as well as the information and advocacy you need. Those contacts may or may not be your closest friends. In fact—as I mentioned earlier—some argue that acquaintances can be more helpful than close friends in providing leads, because they take you into a sphere of people with whom you don't have regular contact.[1] "The strength of weak ties," as Veronica suggests. (Bear that in mind the next time you serve on a volunteer board with someone you like but who is not a close friend.) Regardless, you will need contacts to help you out. As Cassandra, that mother from Texas who has held a series of part-time jobs suggests, "I have a great network of friends and past colleagues who know that I most enjoy part-time, flexible consulting projects, and they are always on the lookout for me." Don't go it alone.

Option One: Start with Your Current Employer (If You Have One)

Why begin with your present boss? Because that employer knows your skills and has got a vested interest in keeping you on. This holds true whether you need a new set of benefits or an altered schedule, either of which may constitute family-friendly work for you.

In fact, given your needs, making your work more family-friendly may simply be a matter of getting more employer-backed support. One human resources manager to whom I spoke said she often finds that an employee's sudden inability to get work done comes down to seemingly insurmountable challenges she is facing at home. If you are facing challenges with regard to child care, meeting health care or other financial needs, your employer may be able to offer support. Approach the person or department responsible for staffing and benefits and see what options exist that may better support your needs. If, for example, your employer has implemented what is known as cafeteria benefits, you may be able to "purchase" additional benefits based on salary and tenure. Sometimes an employer may offer more than one health insurance policy or point you toward other programs or policies that you might not have considered. They might, for example, be able to suggest child-care resources that they support. They might be able to link you up to people within the organization who have faced similar challenges. If your company has an Intranet, research your options there and/or consult your company handbook. Don't underestimate the support your company and those within it may be able to provide.

But if that help is not enough, if based on your needs and your skills, you've determined that you and your family will be better served by a new job arrangement than a new benefit or added financial support, a current employer is still probably the best starting point. That employer knows your skills and will probably be more confident than a new employer in your ability to get the job done. In Chapter 16, I'll discuss how to approach your employer about altering your arrangement. That may mean restructuring your job so that you have less interaction with clients, less management responsibilities, or other alterations that make your job more accommodating of your needs. And if you find, as you go through that process, that altering your job responsibilities is not viable, you may be able to find a new position within your employer that better tolerates nontraditional schedules. Finding that position may take work, but it may be possible if you've developed a strong reputation and network within your organization.

If you do take that route, ask yourself which if any work-content and transferable skills are strong enough and relevant enough to other areas or company divisions. Check the company Intranet or job board to see if any positions are available, a possibility particularly if your company is large. Some companies even have job share boards, for example. Also research your options among trusted colleagues. Talk with your human resources department. Most large companies will often hire from within before advertising a position to the public. As you look into making an internal move, familiarize yourself with your company's policy for job changes. Find out the amount of time required to work in one area before you can switch to another. Ask about any educational or training prerequisites for advancing. Determine if you must get approval from your manager. Realize, as you do research, that you are taking risks here. In looking, you are telling your employer that your job no longer works. So be sure you've investigated flexible options within your current role first. Remember too that a strong network within your company and relevant skills will help keep the transition smooth—so will a company large enough to support internal moves.

That's, at least, the experience of Rachel, a mother to two from New York and training manager with a large telecommunications company. She decided after maternity leave for her second child that her position would demand too much time away from her children. With the support of her supervisor, she looked internally for another position, applying to some 30 positions via her company's Web site. For those positions, only three people called her, two of whom disqualified her based on the fact that her skills set didn't match up. The third—who worked with and had an endorsement from Rachel's friend and former colleague—offered Rachel the job.

Option Two: Approach a New Employer

If a current employer cannot meet your needs, your next best bet to getting a nontraditional arrangement is to move one step out. Try to find a job—based on networking through contacts you trust—that draws on your strongest transferable and work-content skills. This will probably mean finding a job in a similar line of work that you do now or once did. If, for example, you are a creative director at an advertising firm, you could move to the "client side" in another industry that is more accommodating to the needs you have. Find out through your network, professional organizations, or even the Web about what options exist. What responsibilities do those jobs have? How do the tasks vary from what you do now in the industry you're in? What added demands would you face? Remember, the more convinced the prospective employer is of your skills, the better chance you'll have in getting the arrangement you seek. So if you use your network to find someone who values your work based on work you've done before, you'll probably have better luck.

If your skills qualify, you also can put your name with recruiters. A number of recruiters specialize in getting people jobs on alternative arrangements. Some of these, however, specialize in particular fields, as they believe that some fields (ones that require a lot of client contact, such as some sales jobs, for example) don't sustain some nontraditional work arrangements such as part-time well. You may use a traditional recruiting firm to get family-friendly work, but you need to be willing to work or at least consider working on traditional terms first. If you are willing only to work on nontraditional terms, particularly a shortened week, most recruiters will recommend that you use your own network instead.

When opportunities do come up, don't turn down an interview because you think it unlikely they'll accept your terms or don't turn them down because you feel your skills overqualify you for the job.

Some Flexible Arrangement Recruiting and Placement Agencies

• Flexible Resources at *www.flexibleresources.com*

• FlexTime Solutions at *www.flextimesolutions.com*

• Woman's work at *www.womans-work.com*

• Snag a Job at *www.snagajob.com* (part-time employment)

• Unicru at *www.unicru.com* (hourly jobs)

• *www.jobsharing.com* (job-sharing)

• *www.a2zmoonlighter.com* (freelance work)

Give the opportunity a chance to play out. Once more, stronger than required skills may be what the employer needs to give you the job on the terms that you seek. Think about it: Who would you instinctively trust more to work as an advertising copywriter on a part-time basis: someone who has written advertising copy for years or someone who has written magazine articles in the past? And who do you think will do a better job? Remember Claire, the woman in the introduction to this book who's worked in magazines her entire career? When she spreads the word among contacts that she's looking for work, the job that comes up often is one for which feels she is overqualified. But she doesn't turn it down for that. Instead, she looks at that situation as an opportunity to overdeliver, reinforcing for the employer that she is an employee worth the terms that *she* asks, because she can do the work that *they* ask. This is a sound approach, particularly if you will be charging by the hour or working limited hours, as you will need to be using your work time, above all, to produce. Your employer won't want you using that work time primarily to learn your craft. Likewise, if you're working from home

without the support of co-workers, you probably won't be in a position to benefit from much on-site training. You better have those
skills from the outset.

Again as you do look around, be as discreet as possible. You don't
want your current employer to sense you're looking around and
then risk losing your job.

Option Three: Use Your Skills for Another Profession

If your profession no longer satisfies you, it can't afford you with the
work–life accommodations you need, or you've been out of the
workforce so long that you don't have a profession to speak of,
think about your strongest skills and interests. Which interests rank
top? Are there ways you can apply some of your strongest work-
content and transferable skills to fields that relate to those interests?
If journalism has always interested you and you are a doctor, for example, could you apply your medical knowledge in journalism? In
what capacity would that be? Could you consult, work in-house, or
freelance with your skills—if not immediately, then down the line?
Could you command the benefits or income you need?

If you're looking for a new profession, you'll need to do a lot of
research before you actively go after a job. You'll need to get out
your bookmark again and look at your strongest skills and knowledge areas and begin to consider where you might apply them. To
research your options and their relative family-friendliness, you'll
need to draw on your own knowledge and the knowledge of people
in your listed networks. You'll need to seek out colleagues, friends,
neighbors, parents of your children's friends, former classmates, and
alumnae. Like Lonnie, whom you read about earlier, you'll need to
find people who work in fields that interest you and then ask them

```
┌─────────────────────────────────────────────────────────┐
│            Thinking About Direct Sales?                   │
│                                                           │
│ Realize that if you haven't worked for a long time, you lack strong work-content │
│ skills, but you're good in sales, a strong network may provide the leverage you │
│ need to get certain types of jobs. Direct sales jobs—that includes working as a │
│ distributor, rep, or consultant who may sell products at company sites, through │
│ parties, at home, on the phone or via e-mail—can be ideal for women reenter- │
│ ing the job market who have strong sales skills and a good network. In fact, di- │
│ rect sales doubled from 1991–2000 to about 25 billion; and 73% of that sales │
│ is women.* If you think you might want to be one of them, visit The Direct Sell- │
│ ing Association to find out more (www.dsa.org). │
│                                                           │
│                                                           │
│ *Direct Selling Association, 2001 Growth and Outlook Survey, (Washington, DC: 2001). Sta- │
│   tistics available at: www.dsa.org/research/00numbers.htm; accessed on: April 3, 2003. │
└─────────────────────────────────────────────────────────┘
```

if they can think of areas in which your skills apply. You'll need to find out what those jobs are, what kind of hours they demand, who succeeds at them, and whether the arrangement you seek is possible in that line of work. You'll need to call them up and say, "I'm really interested in what you do, I wonder if I might arrange a time to talk for 15 to 20 minutes about what you do. The reason is I'd love to see whether there's a way my skills might apply to your field." If, when you do talk to them, they see an area where your skills might fit, ask them if they know anyone who might be able and willing to provide you a little more information. Ask if your contact would be willing to let you use her name when you call.

When you talk to the person your contact referred you to, you'll want to get a lot of information. You'll want to ask how she got in her position and what qualifications she needed. You'll want to ask how her job works for her and what challenges she faces. You'll want to ask whether such a position, in her view, can support nontraditional arrangements. You'll want to see how it meshes with parenting.

If, after pursuing such a process, you do decide that you want to pursue an entirely new profession for which you have no work-content skills, proceed prudently. "Think ahead and then backtrack, asking, what do I need to do to get there?" advises Richard Diedrich, a consulting psychologist. If, for example, your desired position is senior enough to attract executive recruiters, talk to some. They could be helpful in clarifying what you need to do to get from A to B. If your desired position is not that senior, get an appointment with a HR professional or the equivalent executive in the field that interests you. Ask these executives what they would need to see on your résumé for you to be a potential candidate. Then ask yourself what time frame is realistic to get those qualifications and/ or skills, given your responsibilities as a mother. What needs are you willing to leave unmet to get there? What needs must be met? If working part-time, flexible hours, or telecommuting is a priority for you, how viable is that in the line of work that you are pursuing?

If This Book Is Not Enough

If all this sounds well and good, but frankly you still have no idea what you want, or what I've provided is not enough to set you off on your search, you may need to seek out more career books. (*What Color Is Your Parachute?* by Richard Bolles is a good place to start.) You can also do what experts like Diedrich asks his clients to do: Think about your life on a much larger scale. Think about what has been most significant in your life. How do you define yourself? What would you want people to say about you on the day you retire? What roles, characteristics, or achievements would you want people to mention when your name comes up in discussion? What life events or experiences have been most meaningful to you and why? What experiences have been least meaningful or disappointing? Try to answer the question "Who am I?" in ten different ways and then identify which of those answers are most important to you. Take time to reflect.

You also can seek out help from a career coach. You'll find some career coaches, such as Natalie Gahrmann, a New Jersey–based success coach, author, and mother to two children, take a similar tack to Richard Diedrich. "I start my clients on a self-discovery journey to help them understand their core needs, values, priorities, and interests. They discover what's really important to them," says Gahrmann. If you choose this route, do your research on the career coach before you sign on. As when employing any service, first make sure the career coach is reputable.

In addition to career coaches, you also can go for help to the career counseling office of your alma mater or even a local community college. This might be a wise move, particularly if a job change would mean you might need to return to school to get further qualification. Many colleges are happy to help. Just apply that Golden Rule in networking here as you do everywhere else: Be prepared to give back. When relevant, ask if it would be helpful to list yourself as a resource at the college in areas where you think you can help others in their career.

As you go through this process, don't get impatient if the answer takes a while in coming and if the answer changes in time. The process is not easy and requires time to reflect. Keeping a journal may help. Says Seth Moeller, an HR professional, "Whether in a professional counseling session or reading a book, only one person can answer the question: 'Where do you see yourself?'" That person is you.

When you do ultimately get to the stage of applying for jobs in your area of interest, be sure you are prepared to do what it takes to convince them that although you haven't been in this line of work

Skill and Personality Tests

For those of you who are trying to ascertain what career is right for you, career coaches often recommend personality and skill tests.

• Be careful that you use someone qualified to administer such tests, as questions and answers are easily misinterpreted. The Institute for Personality and Ability Testing (IPAT) has some good tests, but they need to be administered by someone qualified.

• Many community colleges can administer personality and skills tests for free as well as assist in the self-discovery processes in other ways, such as offering workshops and counseling. If you're interested, contact a community college near you for help, but realize most community colleges offer assistance in the hope that you will enroll to acquire requisite qualifications for your new career.

• Your alma mater also may help, as will career coaches if you're willing to pay their fee.

• Remember to use test results as part of a process; don't use them as a determining factor as to what you should do with your life.

before, you've got the relevant skills and the commitment. Tell them you've done a lot of soul searching and this is what you want more than anything else. Draw a link between what you've done before and what you're planning to do now. Show them, if relevant, ways in which the same skills apply. Convince them why you'll be good. If you need help in this process, Richard Knowdell has a wonderful exercise that can help you evidence your skills. You can also draw on the worksheet you completed in section 2 on transferable skills.

As you go through this process, you also might want to prepare

Evidencing Your Skills*

If, when it comes to evidencing your skills, you have trouble quantifying or communicating them to an employer, many career books, particularly those that have sections on writing résumés, can help. Richard Knowdell has an exercise called "For Instances," found in his *Motivated Skills Manual*, that can help. I like it because it tends to incorporate all of your skills and provide focus. Here's how it works.

FOR INSTANCES

Once you know the skills you are best at and most enjoy using, you need to be able to convince employers of your actual achievement in these areas, to cite job-relevant examples of your effectiveness. These examples can draw on two kinds of qualifying experience: direct and related.

Direct qualifying experience is anything that obviously or formally supports your candidacy for a job. Related qualifying experience is anything that indirectly or informally supports your candidacy for a job. (Try this exercise with your most job-relevant skills.)

EXAMPLE

• **Skill:** Teaching.

• **Direct qualifying experience:** Student teaching, job experience as a teacher in a public or private school.

• **Related qualifying experience:** Tutoring classmates in your strongest subject, giving a cooking course at your church, leading a how-to group for a scout troop, informally orienting new staff persons to their jobs, demonstrating a product line and its use to the public.

yourself by writing achievement statements for yourself. This, according to some career coaches, entails thinking about the acronym PAR: Projects you've undertaken, Actions you've taken in those projects, and Results you've achieved. Have these ready at the tip of your tongue for your interview process by taking the time to write them down first. Do it now, if you like.

Realize, as you pursue this route, that your current skills set will directly influence how quickly and effectively you can transition into your desired role. As the experiences of Kristi, Claire, and Cassandra suggest, you probably will be able to make the transition more quickly and effectively if you draw primarily on skills—work-content and transferable—that you already have. If you don't, you may have a harder task initially in getting terms you want.

Of course, the stronger your transferable skills and professional status, the less pivotal those work-content skills may be. Remember Lonnie, the lawyer mentioned earlier in this book? She thinks law is one of the best-kept secrets in getting a wide range of work even though one might not be using one's law degree. But is it any wonder, given the high regard with which a law degree is held and the high level of skills the profession requires? Likewise, someone who holds an MBA might pursue a job she's never done, but that degree may make her appealing nonetheless. And don't let people deter you because they think you might be overqualified for the job. "Don't let your MBA get in the way," says Jane, pointing to the obstacles that a high level of experience or a degree may present. She should know. When she made that switch from investment banking into high-end travel, she was told throughout her search process that she was overqualified for jobs that would have given her the training to switch careers. As a result, she spent a long time trying to convince her prospective employer, through persistent checking in, that high-end travel was what she wanted more than anything else, and she took particular pains to show them how her skills set could apply. Eventually, that employer took her on. After more than a year

Family-Friendly for Those with Few Skills or Little Education

The sad truth is that if you have few skills, particularly as far as qualifications such as education are concerned, you are going to have a much harder time getting family-friendly work. Again and again, surveys find that the one category of workers who often miss out on family-friendly benefits is blue-collar workers.*

If you have few skills or only a high-school education, you, sadly, have much less leverage in securing a family-friendly arrangement. Moreover, legislation does little to protect you in terms of hours you work. Overtime can feel obligatory and attending school functions impossible. You may have little access to affordable child care as employer-sponsored child care often is not available to lower-income women. Caring for a sick child may mean using your precious few vacation days.

Information like that won't help you. But what may help you is to first try as hard as you can to get further education or training (through your employer, if viable). Getting your employer to invest in you—your training and education—is the best job security you'll get, as difficult as the time commitment may be.

Second, get support at work and off. Unions, for example, can give you leverage as far as getting leave and costly benefits that your skills alone won't secure. As I was writing this book, Ford Motor Company was in the midst of developing a benefits program that included 24-hour, on-site child care that equally supported hourly and blue-collar workers—a rarity among most corporations. Who was behind that initiative? The United Auto Workers. Colleagues at work can help as well by providing some leverage and support that you otherwise wouldn't get. As you may recall, one factory worker whom I interviewed calls her work "very" family-friendly because colleagues trade shifts when needs demand, an initiative completely run and administered by employees alone.

*In one University of Cincinnati survey conducted in 1998, 500 randomly selected respondents from Ohio were shown 12 workplace benefits and asked to check those available to them in there, she moved on to open a business for herself, a position she considers extremely family-friendly now.

Making the Investment

To get her family-friendly arrangement—her own business—in a different line of work, Jane obviously put in some time first. She's not alone. If you don't have the work-content skills that your prospective field requires, you may have to consider doing the same. If that position does require such an investment, you have to determine whether you have enough flexibility to arrange your life to get those skills, whether through further education, training, or on-the-job experience. You have to sit down and think about the time acquiring such skills will take and whether you and your family can handle the resulting demands. You may, for example, need to get your real estate license or your nursing degree. Is your interest strong enough to dedicate the time and make the sacrifices that requires? If you feel that you can manage to take this route—given your financial demands and your children's needs—prepare yourself and your family. Explain to your family how important the switch is for you. Explain it will take some juggling on everyone's part, and that you hope, in the end, they and you will be much better off as a result. Tell them it's for a finite period of time.

Realize too that if you do take this route, the fact that you also have to care for children may slow the rate at which you advance. School may take longer if you have to simultaneously care for children. Factor that in. And just because you have children, that you're older, or have other impressive qualifications to your name, doesn't mean you won't have to put in the time like everyone else. Valerie, a former executive at a New York City–based publishing company and now mother of two, decided to get out of publishing to become a nurse. When her first child was still a toddler, she went back to college to get another degree. When she got out, she still had to work the night shift for six months like every other new hire. It was particularly hard because her husband was a management consultant and gone three nights a week, so they temporarily had to have an overnight caretaker for their child. It was a grueling six months, but now she does what she loves and works part-time.

The other point to bear in mind is that some family-friendly jobs, by their nature, won't require you to put in time. They have fewer barriers to entry and are offered on terms that may already meet your need. If, for example, you decide that being a salesperson in a clothing shop meets your needs, you may be able to get that job simply based on the fact that you can sell (a transferable skill) and that you have an interest or knowledge of retail. You also may be able to get that job on the terms that you want, such as part-time, due to the fact that it's common to get that work in that area on those terms. In fact, a lot of fields that are dominated by women offer nontraditional arrangements almost as a norm, whether part-time, nonstandard hours, reduced hours, or shift work. (Just look at the leading occupations of employed women.) So if you pursue one of those industries for which your desired work–life benefit is common, you'll no doubt have a better chance of getting it. Realize too, however, that many of these positions are among the lower paid.

Consider, too, the state of the economy in your search. In good times, jobs are more plentiful, so provided you qualify, you may

Leading Occupations of Employed Women*

- Managers and administrators

- Secretaries

- Cashiers

- Sales supervisors and proprietors

- Registered nurses

- Elementary school teachers

- Nursing aides and orderlies

- Waiters and waitresses

- Sales workers—retail and personal

- Receptionists

*Bureau of Labor Statistics, *Employment Projections* (Washington, DC: U.S. Department of Labor, 2001).

have an easier time getting a job that offers employer-sponsored benefits. Likewise, if you qualify for a position where the level of skill and the strength of the economy make it difficult to fill, you may have more leverage in negotiating a family-friendly arrangement. Last, if you're in a growing occupation that demands a strong level of skills, you could use that positioning to your advantage. Work in technology, health, and special needs are all growing areas that often can support nontraditional arrangements. If your interests and skills apply to one of the following fastest-growing occupations, you may be in luck.

Fastest Growing Occupations, 2000–2010*

• Computer software engineers, applications

• Computer support specialists

• Computer software engineers, systems software

• Network and computer systems administrators

• Network systems and data communications

• Network systems and data communications analysts

• Desktop publishers

• Database administrators

• Personal and home care aides

• Computer systems analysts

• Medical assistants

• Social and human service assistants

• Physician assistants

• Medical records and health information technicians

• Computer and information systems managers

• Home health aides

• Physical therapist aides

• Occupational therapist aides

• Physical therapist assistants

• Audiologists

- Fitness trainers and aerobics instructors

- Computer and information scientists, research

- Veterinary assistants and laboratory animal caretakers

- Occupational therapist assistants

- Veterinary technologists and technicians

- Speech-language pathologists

- Mental health and substance abuse social workers

- Dental assistants

- Dental hygienists

- Special-education teachers, preschool, kindergarten, and elementary school

- Pharmacy technicians

*Bureau of Labor Statistics, *Employment Projections*, (Washington, DC: Department of Labor, 2001).

One little aside here is that Department of Labor research shows that service-producing businesses tend, on the whole, to do better in times of recession than goods-producing businesses, as does private education, social services, health services and local government. These industries also tend to employ large numbers of women, whereas goods-producing businesses tend to employ higher proportions of men. That's why women tend to fare better in times of recession than men. So, if the economy is in recession and you're concerned about the security of your job, history suggests that you may be better off in one of these sectors if your skills match.

But those asides shouldn't determine in which industry you ultimately decide to work. If you are making the commitment to a new career or entering a new field, your priority should rest on drawing on your strongest skills and on knowledge that interests you. In the words of Helen, an Internet executive who moved to Chicago (husband and children in tow) to get her graduate business degree: "You will feel all the time apart from the children as a sacrifice so you must be doing something you feel is worth that."

Real Mother Recap

If you've taken the time to do these exercises, you should have a better idea of your strengths and skills. The more closely aligned your skills to your job, the easier time you'll have getting it on the terms you want. If you decide that you want to pursue a line of work that draws on vastly different work-content skills, proceed prudently. Find out what skills are necessary for the job you seek. Figure out what's needed to get those skills and how that will affect the demands that you face. Talk to recruiters, if relevant, or people in similar lines of work. And when you do look at a particular job or field, be sure to look around you and see how many mothers fill those roles. Is it male-dominated? And if so, why? If it is, make certain you have the level of skills that enable you to ultimately do the job on the terms you want.

If you need more help: Pick up a copy of *What Color Is Your Parachute?* by Richard Bolles.

15

Assess the Job

I have compromised to have a tremendous amount of flexibility as well as financial reward. And, I might add, I wouldn't do it any other way right now, because my kids are my priority.

—MAGGIE

MAGGIE

Maggie is one of those people who can put you at ease through a single word, who knows the power of praise in changing the dynamics of an exchange. "Would you mind if I interview you?" I asked via e-mail one afternoon. "I'd be honored," she replied, setting the bar for the quality of the interview I now must conduct.

But find out a little more about Maggie's work experience, and her ability comes as no surprise. Maggie is an executive recruiter in the retail business. She works from home, part-time, conducting her searches through picking up the phone and telling people she hasn't met about jobs they may or may not want. It's a sales job of sorts, where a few well-chosen words can make all the difference in getting a stranger not to hang up.

Maggie was not always in this role, but the skills and knowledge she has accumulated along the way clearly have prepared her well. Maggie began her career in a highly competitive training program at a major clothing retail chain. But after four years, the company underwent a leveraged buyout and "everything came to a screeching halt in terms of promotion," she says. So she left, but not without a good knowledge of retail under her belt.

She then set up a custom, computer-designed, swimwear store (where can there possibly be greater demand for someone who can make you feel better about yourself than when standing naked before a mirror?). But in the summer and spring, Maggie was working six to seven days a week. Customers came back because they wanted her and no one else. Long term, she decided, that job wouldn't work. "I was very conscious of how it was going to impact my life."

The reason for her concern was that Maggie was soon to be married and she wanted to hold a job that could work with having children. She felt certain running her swimwear shop would not. So she thought about her skills and her knowledge and tried to come up with a way to apply them that would allow her to work from home. Executive recruiting was where she ended up.

For the first two years, Maggie worked for a major executive recruiting firm. Then she followed her boss, Michael, to a smaller firm, "all the time knowing I could eventually do this career from home." She finally was working three days at work and two at home. "I felt like I had almost become indispensable to Michael. I knew I could call the shots." After her second child was born, she decided the security of her husband's income and her own experience enabled her to set out to do what she had planned. She went freelance, working part-time, entirely from home.

Although she calls her job "extremely" family-friendly, Maggie doesn't feel her job is completely fulfilling on a professional level. She is not making use of all of her skills. Some nights last summer she lay awake wondering what she was doing with her life. But, in the end, she couldn't find a compelling alternative. At senior corporate executive levels, retail is not family-friendly, she says. "People work very hard," she says, pointing out that the industry is dominated by men. "I think I have another business inside me," she concedes, but she doesn't know what.

In the meantime, her business provides financial security, flexibility, and a lifeline into a network and an industry to which she's remained committed her entire career. She also derives satisfaction from the fact that she can draw a good income while working on terms that she sets. She sees herself, after all, as a paid worker, not as a full-time, stay-at-home mom. Her job may not be ideal, but it meets her most important needs and draws on the strength of some of her skills. For now, she says, "There's nothing pulling me great enough to give up what I get from my kids."

After you think you've determined the field and occupation and perhaps even employer that interests you, you want to assess how well they are going to meet your individual needs. That's what this chapter is about.

Had you, for example, asked Maggie 10 years ago what she would like to be doing by her late 30s, being a mother probably would have featured somewhere in her response. Working a defined number of hours also may have found a place. Being an executive recruiter almost certainly would not have.

Maggie, like many mothers who hold work that they deem to be family-friendly, chose her job not because it was her end-all job, but because she knew, based on her knowledge of that line of work, that she ultimately could leverage her skills to get the arrangement she sought. She also knew what she wanted from her work. So rather than continue to run her own shop or return to an executive job in retail where the hours were long and the senior women few, she pursued executive recruiting. She worked full-out at first, honing and strengthening her skills; and once she felt confident in what she brought to the table, she negotiated family-friendly work. You want to take a similar tack.

Consider the Industry

As you assess whether a particular job will meet your needs, consider the field in which you might work. Maggie, for example, had strong retail skills but she also believed, based on her experience, that retail at senior levels would not support her needs. Executive recruiting, she saw, could support her needs through a telecommuting arrangement. So she used her knowledge of retail and her skills to move into that field.

Maggie was more shrewd than she may have realized. According to the Families and Work Institute's *1998 Business Work-Life Study,* industry is the most frequent predictor of work–life support. And guess what? Wholesale and retail trades emerge as least generous time and time again.[1] That does not mean you won't find family-friendly retailers. Some are extremely sensitive to their employees' needs. But as you go through this process, you, too, need to ask yourself what is the standard against which employers and employees in a particular industry hold themselves? What is typical practice? Do typical hours in that industry, particularly in the job that you seek, preclude employees from having much time for their family? Is part-time, for example, common or rare? What type of work–life benefits are commonly available? Thinking about your field and/or industry at this level is important, as employers give more thought to common practice than you might think. In fact, "benchmarking," by which the company tries to ascertain where its pay-and-benefits structure falls next to the competition, is common among big employers. If, for example, it's common practice for the competition to offer child-care support, you have a better shot of getting it yourself. If it's rare, you'll have a hard time finding it yourself. And if the benefit or arrangement requires significant employer expenditure, negotiating it at an employer will be near impossible, no matter how convinced the employer of your skills.

Think Specifically About the Benefits and Arrangements *You* Need

In studies, finance often stands out as among the most generous fields, whereas wholesale and retail trades emerge as among the least generous.[2] But how either of those industries works for you depends on what you need. The finance industry, for example, may be very generous when it comes to benefits like child care, but part-time work as an analyst at a top firm will probably be much harder to secure than a part-time sales position in a large retail shop. So think about the position you would hold in that industry as well. Given your skills and the demands of your position, how viable is it to get the arrangement or benefits you need in that industry? Is it realistic to expect any employer to give you what you want given your job? Draw from the knowledge of people who hold that level in your field and from your own experience if relevant. What kind of demands does the job create?

Realize, too, that exceptions exist. Many mothers, for example, told me that under no circumstances could the law profession meet their needs. It was absolutely *not* a family-friendly profession, they said. Yet I found a handful of women in law who had managed to find a unique position at a law firm that was, they thought "extremely" family-friendly. Once more, many women to whom I spoke pioneered the family-friendly policies at their jobs. Before them, the company would not have been called family-friendly at all. So use industry as an overall gauge, but don't set its overall practices as hard-and-fast rules.

Research the Company

The approach of your prospective company also is key to determining how well your job can support your needs. So if you're looking for family-friendly benefits or arrangements, you need to take a close look at the employer and its approach toward work–life issues. You can start by doing some research even before you set foot through the company door. Visit the company Web site. Does the company position itself as family-friendly? Has it won any awards? Is it on *Fortune* magazine's list of the Best Companies to Work For? Has it ever made *Working Mother* magazine's list of the country's most family-friendly companies? If the company is positioned as family-friendly, you hope it offers some family-friendly arrangements at some levels of the organization. Try to find someone at the organization with whom you can talk. Does she enjoy what she does? Is she satisfied? Does she enjoy the people with whom she works?

Then think specifically about your needs. If, for example, you seek a good benefits package for your spouse and family, financial support for child care, eldercare assistance, and on-site child care, you should find it relatively easy to assess how well an employer can meet those criteria. See what your research digs up. (Do an Internet search on "JP Morgan Chase" and "benefits," for example and you'll see what I mean.) If the company has won family-friendly awards, find out why. Speak to employees you know about the type of work–life financial assistance and benefits the company provides. Before you interview, put in a request to human resources (HR) for any company literature they can offer. Within that, you may find information on the company's work–life policies and benefits, particularly if that company touts itself as being family-friendly. Do that inquiry, by the way, on the premise that, as a job candidate, you want to be as informed as possible about the employer. Don't call them up and say you want to see if you can get what you need. That interview may never materialize.

Once You're Inside the Company

Once you've secured an interview, go a step further. Official policy and media play are certainly not reliable indicators of whether an employer will help address your needs. At least that was the experience of Shannon, a former project manager and single mother in Atlanta, Georgia. She thought her employer had all the right intentions. It had, after all, been listed as one of *Working Mother*'s 100 Best Companies for Working Mothers. The firm reportedly had a generous personal time-off program for employees who had completed one year's service, flexible work arrangements, and mentoring and diversity programs. Shannon thought it ideal. But when her child was still a toddler, she found that the firm fell desperately short.

"[They] tote themselves as having a very publicized work–life balance. I have many examples of this not being the case. . . . Examples exist such as not being able to receive any incoming phone calls from my daughter's day care or from her father to update me on her status. . . . That is why I'm no longer with the firm."

How could there have been such a disparity between her definition of family-friendly and the firm's? Well, the truth is quite easily discerned. The family-friendly arrangements or benefits a company offers do not necessarily answer each employee's needs. Once more, family-friendly perks often don't run uniformly through an organization. In Shannon's case, she got landed with two supervisors who didn't value the corporation's overarching family-friendly ethos. So no matter how family-friendly the company appeared to some, to Shannon it wasn't at all.

Understanding the company and how it works from the inside may help you avoid Shannon's fate. Here's how you can go about assessing it before you sign on.

Know the Company's Position

As a general rule, don't start making overt inquiries on policies and benefits until you have had a chance to sell the employer on your strengths. This holds particularly true when it comes to benefits. If you need some big-ticket benefits—like health care or child-care assistance—you probably won't be able to negotiate these. Instead, you simply want to make sure your employer can provide what you need on this front before you sign on. You should be able to get a good idea of what the company offers here from the company literature. If you can't, don't begin your interview asking what benefits you can get. It's like asking a potential boyfriend how much he makes on the first date. Says one nursery school administrator who was recently interviewing to fill a teaching vacancy at her school, "The first question that so many candidates asked was what are the benefits. It put me off." You want them to want you first. But do get this information before you sign on the dotted line. Some benefits may not be as easy to get as they seem. Company child care, for example, often has limited space, impractical locations for some office branches, bad hours, or unaffordable costs for some employees. Some employers have a menu of benefits for which you may or may not be qualified. But you're probably best off waiting to inquire on those options until you know you're wanted.

Ascertaining a company's approach to flexible work arrangements, however, will probably require a different approach. Think about beginning this assessment some time in the interview process—you hope after you've had a chance to sell them on your strengths but before you start negotiating your job. If they have any written material outlining those policies, read it. If not, ask what they have in the way of work–life policies. If they ask you to elaborate, you might position your question, as one HR person suggests, in a way that shows that you're thinking about their business and how you can best contribute. "In the past I've found that on occasion I do some solitary job tasks very well at home, are you amenable to that?" You can also ask Human Resources what percentage of the workforce uses flexible arrangements. Employees often fail to pursue nontraditional work arrangements—such as telecommuting or part-time—for fear of being taken off the promotion track or of undermining their job security. Bear in mind, too, that if the company is large and those policies are informal, the way flexible arrangements are used throughout the organization can be very inconsistent. "Codification makes it overt and easier to hold managers accountable," says Karen Noble, a Senior Consultant at WFD Consulting, a Boston-based consulting firm. But no written policy does *not* mean that the company is not family-friendly. You just may have a bit more work to do in figuring out if it's family-friendly to you. If by inquiring into these issues, the employer starts second-guessing your commitment, that may be a family-friendly indicator in itself.

Also remember that you sometimes can get a good idea of a company's commitment to work–life policies by asking how long average tenure is at the company and why employees tend to leave. Such a question can open up a discussion on the challenges that the organization faces on this front and the ways in which they've gone about addressing those challenges.

Get a Feel for Your Supervisor

You need a supportive supervisor. Bad bosses are a big reason why employees leave organizations. In fact, my research found that a supportive supervisor was the one consistent finding among the more than 100 women who said they had "very" or "extremely" family-friendly work. "I've just been very fortunate to have an employer that is extremely family-sensitive and supportive," says one attorney from Utah. So try to get a feel for your supervisor or supervisors early on. Look around her office. Is her wall or desk lined with framed certificates or does she have pictures of her family, children's artwork, or any display of outside interests? If so, use that as a launching point of casual discussion when the time feels right. Questions like "Are those your children? Have they ever visited your office?" might trigger a response such as "Oh, of course, they come after school at times or in emergencies." Or "So, you like sailing? Do you get out much?" might trigger the response, "Not with this job."

Don't assume that just because she's a mother she'll be a family-friendly boss. In the interview process, your prospective supervisor might drop other hints. Pay attention to how the supervisor makes you feel in the interview. Do you feel that your supervisor is genuinely interested in you and your experiences, or do you feel like you will be just another head? One woman who was going through a painful divorce said that in her interview process, her prospective supervisor not only said "family comes first" several times but even went so far as to drive an hour and a half to testify in court on her behalf. That may be unusual, but see if the supervisor's words are backed by action among workers. Get a feel for how the team finds working for her. Do staff members feel the supervisor is supportive? What happens when they have to cope with emergencies? What is the rate of turnover in the supervisor's department? Does she provide opportunities for staff development?

Familiarize Yourself with the Corporate Culture

Get a handle on the atmosphere of the company and the division in which you will work. Do you sense an environment of trust? Are people happy? Do workers talk about the place with enthusiasm? Are people friendly in the toilets or elevator? Talk to working mothers and, more specifically, to those within your division. See if you can spend some time at the office before you sign on. Do you see people using the arrangements or benefits to which you too would like access? Does the company feel like a good place to work?

As pointed out by Jim Waller, principal and national director for human resources at Deloitte & Touche (a company that's put a lot of effort toward creating a family-friendly workplace and has been widely recognized for their results), look at whether the company puts greater value toward "input" (hours people put in) or "output" (results). This is art as much as science, Waller suggests, but talking to employees in the organization to find out the hours they work as well as the way they feel about their work should give you an idea here.

As you do this assessment, bear in mind, too, one overarching point borne out by *The 1997 National Study of the Changing Workforce:* How you feel about work matters.[3] That study of close to 3,000 wage and salary workers found that "employees with more difficult, more demanding jobs and less supportive workplaces experience higher levels of negative spillover from work into their lives off the job—jeopardizing their personal and family well-being.[4] What is a high-quality job? Well, according to the report, high-quality jobs are ones that offer autonomy, learning opportunities, meaning, a chance to get ahead and job security. Workplace support is defined to mean flexibility in work arrangements, supervisor support, supportive workplace culture, positive co-worker relations, absence of discrimination, respect in the workplace, and equal opportunity for workers of all backgrounds.[5]

So, as best as you can, try to discern whether your employer will provide that. Given the environment and the job, how happy will you be?

Understand the Structure of the Organization

Look, too, at what kind of environment the structure of the organization supports. A large, multitiered organization that carries a lot of inaccessible authority at the top levels can foster an environment of distrust—and trust is critical if you want to be able to successfully work an alternative arrangement. So, if it is a large organization with top-down management, ascertain whether there is an atmosphere of trust. Is there some sense of autonomy among workers or do they feel managed from the top like puppets? Do managers have enough autonomy that they feel they can support their staff or are they too nervous to make decisions on their own? Realize that companies—particularly large ones with many divisions in different regions—can have subcultures, with different divisions supporting the company's family-friendly policies to varying extents. Those divisions may be autonomous but not family-friendly. Or they may require multiple signatures to get any family-friendly arrangement approved. Ask to see the organization and departmental chart. Know who will make the decisions that directly affect the way you are able to work. A small flat structure is not automatically family-friendly. The start-up, dot-com culture of the 1990s was also one in which many worked liked dogs.

See How Well You Fit into That Culture

Look at those self-management skills of yours again as well as your professional values. What kind of worker are you? In what kind of work environment do you thrive? Does this particular company environment match your self-management skills? Do you see like-minded people? "Are you going into a culture where they wear overtime on their sleeves like badges?" asks Helen, a divorced mother of two boys from Utah. If, for example, you ask prospective colleagues of their proudest professional accomplishments and the answer is that all-nighter a few months back, that's a signal in itself.

Understand the Assessment and Review Processes

Assess and review both company policy and employee performance. "Finding out what an employer inspects can help you determine what it expects," says Waller. Ask them what they measure when they look at how successfully the company is being run. Ask them how they measure the success of employees. On what basis do they make decisions on advancement? Is there a fast track—as often is the case in law, academics, and finance—that employees have to pursue if they want to advance? How is that fast track defined? Also understand the review process and who's involved.

Understand the Nature of Your Job and Employer Expectations

As I've mentioned before, some jobs are entirely collaborative. Some are better performed when working alone. Some carry responsibilities that carry strict deadlines, some are not time-sensitive at all. Some require customer interface. Some require constant client management. All those characteristics will affect the way in which you do your job—such as whether you need to work on-site for regular hours or whether you can work with a degree of flexible scheduling or some days at home. You have to know your job enough to get a sense of what kind of responsibilities it carries and the employer's expectations of how they can best be carried out. Your prospective employer should be able to help you understand that. Ask, for example, about a typical day. What are the main functions of the job? What are the end objectives? If you were performing really well in that job, what would you be achieving? With whom would you be working? Again, how autonomous is the job?

Determine How Many Women Are in Senior Positions

After company size and industry, the number of top executive positions filled by women is the third most frequent predictor of the level of a company's work–life support.[6] So, if you don't see a lot of women in senior positions, take note. There are probably fewer people grappling with your same work–life issues who have the power and desire to introduce change. Investment banking, for example, is notorious for not being able to meet the terms that most mothers need (yes, there are exceptions). And many women I interviewed who held jobs in these fields said they only needed to look at the paucity of mothers in senior levels of this field to see that truth born out. "There are very few senior women or mothers in my office. I work in a male-dominated industry," says one portfolio manager from Chicago, who calls her job only "somewhat" family-friendly. "A lot of employers have old-school thinking about part-time work and working from home. It's a male-dominated field," says a civil-environmental engineer from California. Note, too, whether any of the women in senior positions are taking advantage of flexible work arrangements. Note whether any men are as well. Both can be encouraging signs that the employer supports flexible arrangements.

Don't, by the way, confuse the number of women in senior positions with the number of women overall. The reason is that a large proportion of women in an industry is not always a clear indicator of work–life support.[7] While a large proportion of women is helpful in that it gives you a large pool of women from whom you can draw information, it doesn't mean you're necessarily more likely to get your needs met. It depends on what needs you have.

Where Does All This Leave You?

Get out that bookmark again and look at your needs, your skills, and possibly your interests to see whether your employer can support those. Consider your self-management skills and professional needs to see how well they mesh with the culture of your organization. Think about the type of job that you'll be doing, the people with whom you'll be working, and the supervisor to whom you'll have to answer. Look at the culture of the organization as a whole—how formal is it and how happy are the employees within your division? Look at what type of work–life policies are available and how often they are used. Know, above all, whether your demands are viable.

Real Mother Recap

So there you have it: The process you'll undertake for identifying and assessing how well you think a potential job will meet your current needs. That process will involve looking at the industry, the company culture, the management style, the supervisor, the number of women at the top, the demands of the job itself, and how well you fit in. Should you hold or find a job that could be molded into an arrangement that meets your needs, read on! The next chapter is about negotiating an arrangement that works.

If you need more information: The Families and Work Institute has done a lot of research on family-friendly workplaces (www.familiesandwork.org).

16

Negotiate Family-Friendly Work

I wouldn't have been given this opportunity if I didn't have my track record.

—KYLIE

KYLIE

Kylie is a mother to one and public relations executive who works in Nevada. Her company does employ women, but most are predominantly young and some recently married. Because of that, she has been the first in most every work–life request she's set forth. When she took maternity leave, she was the first to do so in 28 years. "The company's small. So I was lucky to get that," she says of the fact that half her leave was paid. When she returned, the company had a lock installed in a conference room so she could have a place to express her milk. "I wanted to be able to nurse my child and the rest room didn't work." When she felt she was not giving the time she needed to her child, she secured a part-time arrangement.

Kylie, like many of the women in this book, is nothing short of a pioneer. Maternity leave, nursing on-site, and part-time work all have been experiments for her and her company. And so far, they've worked. "They've rewritten the whole maternity-leave policy to clarify several items and expanded adoption policy as well. I'm proud to have been a part of that," she says. Her part-time arrangement has had a similar effect. "I felt a lot of pressure going into it," she says of her proposal to go part-time. "I tried to come up with a good deal for my employer, my clients, and myself."

Her proposal was not an easy one to make. When she returned, she worked full-time for four months. With an hour's commute, she found the time commitment too much. She approached her supervisor, laying out how she would handle her responsibilities and why it would work. "I was told no way."

They talked. Kylie said she couldn't understand why she couldn't go part-time. We need you here, they said. You have staff reporting to you and you need client contact. She persisted. On learning she wanted to go part-time, one of her clients even said she would make a fuss if Kylie were turned down. Eventually, a compromise was made.

"We agreed in the middle," she says. "I no longer have supervisory responsibilities, just client contact." She does, however, get to work three days a week and some of that time is spent working from home. "I wouldn't have been given this opportunity if I didn't have my track record," she says.

But there's another reason for her success: the head partner. "When his own wife had a child, her employer would not give her flexibility. She ended up leaving," she says. "I think our partner now is pretty proud."

In fact, management now knows arrangements like hers can work when the applicant has the skills and the arrangement is executed well. "They see it succeeding," she says. "There's a reward. No one else has to pick up slack from what I'm not doing. I'm still active on management, probably more so. I don't have any offi-

cial supervisory roles. But I'm still quite active in performance reviews."

Her clients, too, continue to be good advocates. "They are very supportive," she says. And for a public relations executive, that clearly counts.

Once you have a job or are relatively convinced that you've got the job, that's the time to start thinking about negotiating it on terms that are better for you. If you have worked in your position for some time, you have an easier task, not only because the employer should be confident of your skills but also because you have a clearer idea of the job's demands. You know what its responsibilities are.

Yes, women do get jobs on alternative arrangements without having worked at the company first. As I've mentioned before, a strong skills set that clearly answers the demands of the job helps, even if overqualifying you for the job. "I have always had to propose my arrangement and usually my boss will go for it because they would like me to work for them," says Cassandra, a mother of two from Texas who's held a string of nontraditional positions. "I could definitely add value. I didn't overpromise. I always took jobs where I knew I could deliver," says Eve who has also held a string of family-friendly positions at companies in marketing.

A strong network within the company can help as well, particularly if it reaches into the upper levels of management. The people with whom Samantha first worked and with whom she developed good relationships at her company are now not only in middle management but in top positions as well. That network provides her with key alliances for securing work—and for maintaining support.

Equally important in getting nontraditional arrangements is being so familiar with the job and its demands that you know how you can make it work within the arrangement you seek. You're better equipped to make this judgment if you've been in the position or a similar position for some time.

Negotiating Benefits for a New Job

Big-ticket benefits that require significant employer expenditure, like health care and child care, tend not to be negotiable. But benefits that do not cost significant capital expenditure may be negotiable. Two of these items are

• **Compensation:** Salary, company shares, and bonuses.

• **Leave:** Medical leave, sick days, personal days and vacation days.

Whether or not these are negotiable will depend on who you are, who your employer is, and how much they want you. Or, as a hiring manager at one company that's widely perceived as "extremely" family-friendly told me, "When people are talented and companies go after them, there's a lot of room for negotiation." A lot of that room can be found in precisely this area.

You may be saying, I'd hardly put financial incentives in my definition of family-friendly. But if you thought about it some more, you might. Most of us do, after all, work to get paid (surprise!) and pay allows us to provide our families with what they need. So while salary is clearly not a benefit, per se, viewing it and other financial incentives as such is helpful. And even though compensation and leave may be negotiable only sometimes, they are topics worth broaching once you've established that the employer wants you. They are part of the "wooing" package. An employer, for example, may pay a little less, but make up for it in other ways, such as shares or paternity leave. So you need to think of this area as potentially negotiable and as part of the family-friendly package.

COMPENSATION

It may, on interviewing, be transparently obvious that you can't negotiate here—you're getting minimum wage, you're desperate for a job, the line of people for this job goes out the door and past the bank where they have nothing in their account. But if you think this area may be negotiable, try broaching it. Bonuses, particularly incentive-based ones, salary, and even reimbursement for incidental costs like commuting might be negotiable in some instances. How much you're paid, by the way, also may be a card to play if people make disparaging remarks about you working less. You don't have to say how much you're paid but you can point out that you've made that trade to get the terms you have. "I'm working less but I'm also making less as well."

FAMILY AND MEDICAL LEAVE

The Family and Medical Leave Act (FMLA) basically requires employers with 50 or more employees to provide 12 weeks of unpaid leave for the birth or adoption of a child or for the serious illness of a child, spouse, parent, or the employee. But depending on an employee's position and employer policy, you may be able to negotiate something better than what the employer is required to give. That may be in the form of unpaid or paid leave. Try to negotiate this leave when it's time (i.e., usually after your third month of pregnancy when you're looking a little fatter than usual), not before. For example, "Yes, I am a woman and you're hiring me and one day I want to have kids. So, will you give me 12 weeks paid then?" *Not a good thing to say.* Bear in mind, too, that the United States is one of the few countries in the developed world that does not mandate paid leave. So paid leave can be hard to find. Once more, many low-income mothers who are eligible to take the mandated 12 weeks of unpaid leave can't afford to take even that. Without a highly desired skills set, they have little negotiating power to change that.

OTHER FORMS OF LEAVE

One chief executive of a small Internet service company told me that while his company couldn't provide large salaries or an impressive collection of paid benefits, one area that he felt he could offer assistance related to leave. For his employees, that assistance might come in the form of sick time, vacation, or personal days off. Some companies also provide paid time off for volunteering—a real asset for mothers who want time to volunteer at their children's school.

For all these benefits, when you discuss them with your employer, try to appear to be taking their interests to heart. "I want to be sure I can do my best to get my work done for you when my children are sick, do you have anything in the way of back-up support in this area?" Or whatever other brown-nosing way you can pose those questions. Some will be hard to pose in that way. "I wan to make sure I'm well rested enough to get my work done, what's your holiday policy?" probably won't fly. Use your judgment above all else.

Last, acknowledge that on this front, as with many other benefits, you often are more likely to get family and medical leave, extend that leave, or get a portion of it paid if you work for a large company.* It is interesting that studies find paternity leave to be one of the few leave benefits that is more common among small companies. So scratch that large company thing for working dads.

*The 2002 survey by the Society of Human Resource Management found that 11% of small companies versus 21% of large companies offered paid maternity leave. SHRM Survey Program, *2002 Benefits Survey* (Alexandria, VA: SHRM, 2002).

But don't let that put you off from inquiring. One human resources professional told me of a woman she knew who turned down a full-time job because she wanted to work part-time. The tragedy, this HR professional said, was that had she asked, she might have gotten the job on the terms she wanted.

When you do ask, however, be confident that they value your skills before you even bring the topic up—and that applies whether you're currently employed or seeking work. "I wouldn't have the opportunity to get through the door if I said I only wanted to work three days," says Annabelle, that consultant and mother to one from Massachusetts who negotiated a part-time job.

Don't try to gauge whether your proposal will be accepted based on the economy either. Yes, if a company is thriving, management may consider introducing new benefits. If hiring talent is extremely competitive, alternative arrangements may be offered as a perk. But how the economy affects your ability to find or negotiate family-friendly arrangements really depends on how well those benefits fall in line with the interests of the business at the time. If you can position your arrangement to match those interests, you're obviously better off. If, for example, the business is facing a downturn and you want to freelance or work fewer hours without benefits, that arrangement might suit an employer just fine. One start-up company that I encountered consistently reduces costs—including employee hours and expenditures—during tough times. For employees there, that may be an ideal time to introduce part-time work. Similarly, as one former CEO of a large public relations firm told me, he was more apt to provide family-friendly perks or benefits to a valued account executive during a downturn, because maintaining that business was all the more important to him then. However, if that person was not performing in that role, he also might be more inclined to let that employee go. For those reasons, as one study suggests, economic conditions are not reliable predictors of work–life benefits.[1]

What all this should enforce for you is the importance of being prepared when you approach an employer about getting family-friendly work. Toward the end of this chapter you'll find a request form designed to help you successfully propose an alternative arrangement. Before you even do that, however, think about what proposing such an arrangement involves.

Understand the Responsibilities of Your Job

Think about the arrangement you'd like and the tasks of your job. How do the two mesh? What supervisory roles, if any, does it have? What collaborative tasks? What tasks are better done alone? What kind of access to information systems do you need? How accessible do you need to be to clients? What tasks do you need to do during core hours? What deadlines are you required to meet? Answers to these questions should begin to give you an idea of whether part or all of your job could be done at home, during off hours, in compressed work weeks or part-time.

Also think about what tasks you are most qualified to do. "Review your strengths and see where you can add value," says Samantha, who works part-time. "I take on projects that others won't do so that I can get a very flexible schedule," says one attorney from Minnesota who works flexible hours, full-time.

If you go part-time, determine which tasks you are prepared to delegate or relinquish. In making that decision, try to be responsible for tasks to which you add clear value and that can realistically be done given the terms you seek. Supervising responsibilities that carry clear deadlines or full-time client coverage may not work. Ask how you will avoid resentment from the people to whom you pass on those tasks. Can you identify people who may look at those tasks as part of a path toward advancement? Can you help train them—a task that will require more time at the onset but will mitigate over time? Can you reduce the number of clients you service or, as Kylie did, drop your supervisory role?

As far as your own professional satisfaction, if you went part-time, would you have to relinquish tasks that provide the most enjoyment in your job? Will your path to advancement stall as a result? How will that make you feel? Can you find other areas in your life that will satisfy those needs?

If, after your review, you find that your full-time job just won't fit into part-time work, can you apply your job skills to another area of the firm? If so, how will you, with your skills, help a manager cope with the demands that her division or job demands? If you take this approach, you obviously will have to have an understanding of the area in which that person works and how your skills fit. Again, if you've worked for the company or in that type of division before, you're better off.

Recall the story of Samantha, who has worked at a pharmaceutical company for many years. She knew after the birth of her first child that she wanted to work part-time from home. The problem was her position would not mesh with part-time work. So she visited every supervisor for whom she felt she could offer relevant skills and said, "This is what I can do for you; let me know if I can take work off your plate." Her strategy worked. Thanks to her strong network within the company and her proven track record, she has consistently worked part-time from home for a variety of departments within her firm. "Solve a problem," she advises. Supervisors with too much work are more likely to bend. That approach, by the way, she says can be used in managing perception as well. "Make sure you and your employer position yourself as reducing another's workload. If you weren't there, someone else would have to do it," says Samantha.

Research

Before you get to the point of approaching someone for alternative work, do your research. Ascertain whether anyone in your company has pursued similar arrangements and what benefits and challenges she faced. "I talked to other women at my company who were working part-time. I had found a number of articles about the benefits of part-time work. I had a lot of information prepared," says Megan, a part-time engineer and mother to three from South Dakota.

Look around you. Does anyone in senior management work an alternative arrangement? Which type of alternative arrangement is most widely used and why? How prevalent are alternative arrangements in your department versus company wide? If you can find people who have used or are using alternative arrangements, talk to them. What challenges did they face in implementing that arrangement? How has the arrangement been received by colleagues? How would they suggest you best proceed if you were to pursue a similar arrangement? What effect do they feel alternative arrangements bear on career advancement?

Look, too, at official company policy for making such requests. Are request and review policies already in place? If so, what does management or human resources feel makes a proposal successful? From whom would you need approval? Is management trained to deal with such requests? What does that training entail and what is management expected to take away? Is there a review policy in place?

Obviously if you are currently working for your employer, these questions will be easier to research. If you have simply been interviewing, however, you'll have to rely more on what you can glean from answers you derived from assessing the company and the culture itself. In addition to that, you can also feel the waters in a way that suggests that you've got their interests at heart. If you want to telecommute, for example, remember the approach that Caroline suggested earlier: "I note you have some people telecommuting here. Is that available at all to new employees? I think better if I'm away from my desk when it comes to certain tasks. What is your position on that?" When you do broach your employer in this context, try to position the enquiry in a way that puts the emphasis on your work.

Also, like Megan, take the time to research the advantages and disadvantages of nontraditional schedules as well as the particular arrangement you seek. A lot of information exists out there about making a case for alternative work. People who are less stressed perform better. People who get work–life support are more committed to their employer. Employment on some alternative terms can lower costs. Alternative arrangements may even increase productivity. Just search the Web and you can find many such studies to document your beliefs or extinguish misconceptions. Comment: "If I let you work part-time, everyone will want to do it." Response: "Actually, if you look at studies of companies where such policies are offered, such as widely recognized studies by William Mercer, you'll find that utilization rates are very low, suggesting that most people don't go after these schedules."[2] Look too at the chapter in this book that relates to the specific arrangement you seek. Be sure your self-management skills match. Anticipate the pitfalls before you come upon them. Know what is right for you and the company and what challenges both will have to overcome.

Position Your Proposal to Make Business Sense

Once you've done your research, be prepared to communicate why your specific arrangement is a good deal for your employer. Do that by framing your proposal in a way that puts the company interests up front. Be prepared to make a compelling case for your arrangement by meeting or even exceeding the company's needs. Perhaps by working from home, you'll be able to better service clients in different time zones, work on necessary tasks without interruption, or allow for an office redesign. Perhaps if you moved your workday an hour back, you'd be better able to focus on important morning tasks performed better without interruption. Perhaps if you worked a compressed workweek, you'd be able to add critical coverage that the company currently lacks. Positioning is key. If you can position your arrangement in a way that results in better work or greater savings, you're better off.

Be Committed to the Company

Try to avoid sounding as if you were giving your employer an ultimatum or that you see your proposed arrangement as an entitlement. "Ask them in a way that you don't turn them off," says the CEO of a small Internet start-up. "Don't say 'contingent upon.' It can't be 'the company owes this to me.' You have to be committed to the company first." You want to communicate that you still will give 100%, and that the quality of your work will not suffer and may even improve as a result.

Get Your Manager, Co-Workers, and Even Clients on Your Side

Realize the arrangement you suggest might not work as you've proposed. Be willing to work with your manager to amend it. Collaboration is important. Be open to discuss all the opportunities and challenges the arrangement creates. Find out if there's anything you can do to make the manager more comfortable with the arrangement or to better support her. Work together.

You also may help your cause if you can get co-workers and clients on your side. Depending on the strength of your relationship with your clients and the closeness and support you have from your team, you may find it to your advantage to get them on board. Vanessa, for example, had full support from her clients and knew she could use that as leverage should the need arise. But proceed carefully here. You want to have a clear idea first of how well your job will translate into the arrangement you seek and where your responsibilities will fall. If by involving them in the process you feel you will get more support, great. But you don't want your client or colleagues to carry doubts about whether the arrangement will work even before you set it up. Consider carefully whom you want to take in your confidence.

Be Prepared to Establish an Evaluation Process

Realize that the arrangement may not end up working once its in place or it may have to be amended or change according to business needs and organizational shifts. Consider suggesting a trial period at first. Throughout that period, somewhere between two to six months, keep abreast of how your arrangement is working for your company and for yourself. "Set performance appraisals," says the CEO of the Internet firm. Establish a review at regular intervals, with greater frequency at the start, and stick to it. "For the first review, don't go more than 60 days," says Noble, the senior consultant, but meet earlier if you deem it necessary. "Encourage managers to check in. Regularly check in with co-workers."

Make a Formal Request

Don't just run the idea by your supervisor. Approach your request professionally. WFD Consulting suggests that a request form can provide structure to your request and help you and your manager address some of the issues just raised. It also can establish between you and your supervisor clear guidelines as to how your work arrangement will be executed. And the manager's signature at the bottom "can be a very critical thing; it signifies agreement between the employee and manager that the arrangement, as detailed in the request, is deemed viable for the business," according to Noble who helped design the request from WFD Consulting.

FLEXIBLE WORK OPTION REQUEST

(Additional pages may be attached to this form if necessary)

I. Employee Information (Employee completes this section)

_____

(name)

_____

(date)

_____

(job title)

_____

(department)

_____

(manager)

_____

(date request submitted to manager)

Flexible Work Option Requested
(circle what applies)

Part-time   Job-sharing (employee must find
                                   partner)

Telecommuting   Compressed workweeks

Flextime   Other _____
                                        (Please specify)

Describe your current schedule and the hours/schedule requested:

days/hours	days/hours	on-site	off-site
(current)	(requested)	(check)	(check)
		☐	☐
_____	_____		
SUNDAY	SUNDAY		

days/hours (current)	days/hours (requested)	on-site (check)	off-site (check)
		☐	☐
_____ MONDAY	_____ MONDAY	☐	☐
_____ TUESDAY	_____ TUESDAY	☐	☐
_____ WEDNESDAY	_____ WEDNESDAY	☐	☐
_____ THURSDAY	_____ THURSDAY	☐	☐
_____ FRIDAY	_____ FRIDAY	☐	☐
_____ SATURDAY	_____ SATURDAY		

Given your proposed schedule, what are the tasks of your job and how will you get them done on a daily basis?

What kind of challenges could your new arrangement trigger with the following groups? (a) external customers, (b) internal customers, (c) co-workers, (d) your manager, (e) others (e.g., project manager)

How do you suggest overcoming any challenges with these groups?

What are the concrete measurable objectives of your job and how do you propose to measure your achievement of them and on what time frame?

If applicable, describe any additional equipment/expense that are required to make this arrangement completely effective. Detail any short- or long-term cost savings that might result from your new schedule.*

II. Request for a Flexible Work Option (manager circles one)

Approved   Declined

If you decline this request, please describe why:

_____

_____
Date

_____
Manager's Signature

_____
Date

_____
Employee's Signature

Effective date of Flexible Work Option

_____
(Beginning)

_____
(End)

* You ideally want your arrangement to either be cost neutral or save money to your firm.

Key Points on Negotiating Family-Friendly Work*

As you go through this process, you also might bear in mind key points for negotiating family-friendly work as recommended by the people at Fannie Mae, a company that is consistently cited as one of the country's leading family-friendly employers. Most of these points repeat what has already been discussed in this book.

• Ask colleagues on flexible work options about their experience.

• Meet with your manager and explain that you'd like to request flexible work options. Include which aspect(s) of flexible work options you're interested in taking advantage of.

• Submit a proposal to your manager outlining your preferred option and explain how the selected option will allow you to contribute to the business without causing a negative impact.

• Explain how your proposed arrangement increases your value on the job.

• Provide a recommended schedule to your manager and remember to be flexible. (There may be times when you may have to work outside of your normal flexible schedule, because of business needs. Remember achieving business goals is the number one priority.)

• In your proposal, describe the potential problems the new arrangement could raise with external customers, internal customers, team or co-workers, and manager. Explain how you'd suggest overcoming any potential problems with these groups.

• Describe the review process you and your manager should use to constructively monitor and improve your flexible work arrangement.

• List any early warning signs that will indicate that the arrangement isn't working.

- If you are proposing a telework schedule, describe what aspects of the position will be done at home and which will be done in the office. Detail any short- or long-term cost savings (for the company) that might result from your new arrangement.

- Meet with appropriate team members and colleagues, if applicable, to discuss the proposed work arrangement and its potential impact on the team.

*From Fannie Mae, 2002.

Real Mother Recap

By now, you should have everything you need to approach an employer about getting **your** family-friendly work. This last step on negotiating is key. For when you approach an employer, you need to position your arrangement, above all, to make business sense. To do that, you need to have enough knowledge to understand the responsibilities of your job. If you can make a good argument that your arrangement will actually benefit your company, you'll have a stronger case. So do all that you can to make your proposal as professional as you can.

If you need more help: www.workoptions.com can provide more information (some at a cost) on negotiating family-friendly work.

17

Maintain Your Family-Friendly Career

As I think I said before, a company is only as family-friendly as the manager you report to. I have truly found that to be the case.
                                                            —RACHEL

RACHEL

Rachel is a mother to two small children in New York. Over the course of my research, she kept me abreast of her work arrangements. In six years, she worked in six different positions—all within the same company. When we first communicated, she was very enthusiastic about how accommodating her company was of employees' needs. "I work for a large corporation, who happens to be very family oriented," she said when we first made contact. "I have held three positions in the past four years and, of these, all of my direct managers have been very understanding of family time. Most of the people I work with have told me they have shared the same good experiences. Our company [also] has wonderful benefits to help with insurance, day care, adoptions aid, etc."

But when I checked in six months later, her situation had changed. "The company promotes itself as family-friendly but it really drills down into the individual units and the manager you report to," she said. "For instance, I worked for a very open-minded woman, also a mom of two. She let us work from home one day a week without justification. Then our company did a re-organization, and I got a new manager—a man in his 40s with a wife who stayed at home. He doesn't get the working mom thing. He revoked our work-at-home day for two months. Then this week he pulled my co-worker and me into a conference room and told us it was reinstated but only if we're working on a large project, and we have to justify it. More trouble than it's worth ac-tually." When Rachel did change her hours, her new manager re-sponded by saying nothing except, "If we need to address it we will."

Nine months later, we corresponded again. "The last year," she said, was "the year of grief." Her new manager, "gnashed his teeth" whenever she worked from home or came in late or left early. But, "I did love my job," she said. Then in May, when her company announced voluntary layoffs, her husband and she de-cided the severance was enough to pay off bills and enable her to stay home with the kids and go back to school. But she didn't have enough seniority to get the package. Then she was told she was be-ing moved from training to compensation. She is now faced with a job change that she is "less than enthusiastic about." But she has been told that her new manager is extremely family-friendly. She has already set one person to work from home two to three days a week. "I don't care what hours you work or where you work them as long as you get the job done," she has been alleged to maintain. "She herself, when her kids were younger, quit working to stay home with them. So she knows a working mother's dilemmas, and I am grateful for that," explains Rachel. "As I think I said be-fore, a company is only as family-friendly as the manager you re-port to. I have truly found that to be the case."

Congratulations. You've got your family-friendly job. Sit back, relax, it's smooth sailing from here. Right? Think again. What I did not anticipate as I interviewed women with family-friendly jobs was the frequency with which their situations would change. A new manager, another child, children matriculating into college, the loss of a spouse's job, a divorce, a corporate downsizing—factors like these were able to transform their situations from "extremely" or "very" family-friendly to "somewhat" or "not at all." No matter how accomplished these women were in consistently securing family-friendly work, transitioning into another job was never an easy task and many had to do it again and again.

When Claire and her husband got divorced, she had to seek out a higher-paying, more secure job that would better support her children and herself. She wanted to work near home but in the end took a job she found through contacts at a large magazine publisher over an hour's commute from her town. She first worked three days a week in place of a woman on maternity leave and when that woman returned, she found another job within that organization on similar terms.

Ellen, the woman introduced at the start of the book, decided she needed to transition from freelancing to a full-time job with benefits so she could support the costs of sending her children to college. In the meantime, she started assisting her spouse in his law practice and added writing coach to her skills.

Eve, the woman in marketing who was called "the master of family-friendly work," left the workforce for a time. She noted:

After the firm downsized in November 2000, I decided to take the following spring and summer off and, at the same time, accepted the position of president-elect with the Junior League. That position has been very challenging—I spearheaded the development of a new three-year strategic plan and have been instrumental in increasing use of e-mail and our Web site within our league. This June, I take over as president for the next 12 months. I have decided not to pursue paid employment during this time. This position affords the same level of satisfaction as a paid job and, frankly, I don't think I could find a job running something on a part-time basis. In fall 2003, I plan on going back to the workforce, perhaps in the public sector."

These women were not so masterful that they never felt compelled to look for new work or didn't endure transitions that were hard to navigate. These women face the same challenges that every employee sometimes endures. But they do adapt.

What are the biggest challenges they face? As Rachel illustrates, unsupportive bosses top the list. They can transform a job from "extremely" family-friendly to "not at all." Why? Because in most organizations, employers expect employees to approach their immediate supervisors first. If a new supervisor is put in place or the current one has a change of heart, a family-friendly arrangement can suddenly be taken away.

What can women do then? The first action you must take is to try to convince the boss that your arrangement is worth the cost. Having been in a situation that seemed to work so well, employees can find that fact easy to accept. But you must learn to make your business case all over again. If it's someone with whom you haven't built up trust or who is not necessarily as receptive to your needs, that task can be difficult at best. But that case must be made. You must show how your arrangement will not adversely affect and may even improve the bottom line of the business you're in. If you continue to get resistance, you should get consultation with a third party, perhaps someone in human resources (HR). "I need your help," is the approach one HR professional recommended. For added support, you can enlist the support of co-workers, colleagues, and even clients if you must.

To avert that situation in the future, you should work hard to maintain your internal network. Having someone backing you internally is what continually helps Samantha when she comes under the supervision of someone new. You have to push for reviews before and after you have those arrangements in place. If those reviews are 360 degrees—that is, get and give evaluations from all around—you'll have more opportunity to join what may be a chorus of voices finding fault with that boss or getting support for work you've done well. As frustrating as it may be, justifying a family-friendly arrangement should not be more trouble than it is worth. If it is, you should question what that worth is.

But sometimes, even those mothers who've held a succession of family-friendly jobs will find that they come against a challenge that is insurmountable given their current arrangement. The new boss can't be convinced. You want or need to be home for your child some afternoons. You can't get the benefits you need. It's then that the really tough decisions begin. Should you make a commitment to leave your job by seeking a transfer within the organization or by looking elsewhere for work? How happy are you in your job? What does your work bring to you and your kids? What do you want out of your life as a parent, as a woman, perhaps even as a spouse? For those who are not struggling to put food on the table, who have skills that can command a decent wage, or have some degree of flexibility because their spouse or partner is gainfully employed, that's when the self-evaluation must begin. So your work does not allow you to be the parent that you want to be. Your boss is not supportive. Your industry is male dominated and fails to acknowledge that workers have lives outside work. In those instances, you have to ask yourself why don't you want to seek something else?

If you are working because you have very real financial needs that only your current arrangement can meet, that is one thing. But what if you won't consider any other work because you feel in your heart that a job with long hours gives you an authority you lack at home? What if you feel your income quantifies your worth like no where else can? What if you work the hours you do simply because that was what you were raised to do? What if you will not cut back or change professions because if your husband won't, neither will you? What if your inability to cope extends much further than work into areas of your personal life?

You have to be honest with yourself. You are not a victim. You have the power to instill change. And if you don't, perhaps you need to reevaluate and perhaps seek advice in other areas of your life that extend outside work, like your relationship with your partner, your children, and yourself.

It is true, taking professional risks by seeking a new employer or changing your role within an organization has to be approached cautiously, particularly in difficult economic times. But as I mentioned earlier, downturns in the economy can create opportunity and market vagaries should not stop you from striving to meet the needs of you and your family.

But don't be misled. You won't find the perfect solution. The work arrangement you ultimately secure probably won't meet all your needs. Significant progress needs to be made before the American workplace is truly family-friendly in all senses of the term. Most jobs are still based around what the author Joan Williams calls an "ideal worker" who can work full-time and overtime without career interruptions and who relies on spousal support to tend to family demands.[1] Earning statistics support that view, with women and men earning comparable income until the ages at which many women start to have children.[2] Once more, the women who seem to have the greatest success in securing family-friendly arrangements that can pay the bills are the ones who put off having children until they have well-honed skills—a delay that puts them having children in their less-fertile 30s.

Yes, we need change. For women to achieve professional parity with men, we need legislation more akin to what California recently did—allow workers to collect partial wages for up to six weeks while they take time off to care for a new baby or a seriously ill family member. We need men to take on more of the child-caring and domestic responsibilities that women bear. We need men in equal numbers to seek out those same accommodations that women seek—paid leave, flexible schedules, part-time work—so they can *share* in the responsibility of caring for the children they have. We need companies to support men and women by recognizing that with nontraditional arrangements these workers can still offer valuable contributions to the workforce. We need affordable child care for children of parents who work long hours at low wages. We need unions to take up the cry of America's workforce—especially blue-collar workers—in trying to bring about better wages, create affordable child care, provide paid leave, and offer more manageable hours and shifts. Until those changes occur, we will continue to make compromises, some of them large.

But we, as women, also can help make our own lives better. We can get the skills and education that make us valuable members of the workforce and give us the leverage we need. We can work to build them where we can, as we go through our lives. We can build our networks at home and at work so that we can get the support we need. We can have the courage and creativity to propose arrangements that work better for us, our employers, and our families. We can strive to actively assess where we are, how we are, and what we want out of life. Are we simply a lawyer or a public relations executive? Or are their other ways that we can find satisfaction in life? If we are caring or artistic, are there areas where we can apply and draw satisfaction from those traits, such as in personal relationships with friends, relatives, or neighbors? Do we have interests that exist outside work? Who or what is defining us? Is it our work? Our neighbors? Is it us?

Last, we need to be open to change and the inherent unpredictability of a course that is just now being forged, a course that differs from those pursued by generations before. Women like Maggie and Samantha and Julia all sometimes lay awake at night wondering where life will lead them next. That is okay. Those feelings of uncertainty are part and parcel of the process of striving to accommodate one's most important needs; they are part of the self-evaluation that needs to take place. "I was jumping off the track, I was angst ridden. It's been a process," says Liz, who now runs strategic planning and investment management part-time for a family-owned business. "You have to know your wants and that they are going to change," says another mother of her career and the decisions she's made. "I searched and searched and searched—and this is the answer for me," says yet another mother of her recent decision to work for herself.

Women like these—women who are part of The Mom Economy—are taking the time to make the hard decisions. They are finding the courage to say no to the promotion if that promotion conflicts with what's important to them. They are forging part-time, at-home, and flexible work schedules. They are starting businesses at twice the rate of men. They are succeeding on terms that they define. "There's a change," as one mother and countless others suggested. It's subtle, but it's there. And the greater that groundswell becomes, the sooner the working landscape that has remained frozen for so long will crack to let more of us secure terms that work for us and our families.

NOTES

Chapter 14

1. This view has been put forward by many. Among works that present a similar view is Malcolm Gladwell, *The Tipping Point* (New York: Little, Brown, 2000).

Chapter 15

1. Ellen Galinsky and James T. Bond, "Executive Summary," *The 1998 Business Work-Life Study: A Sourcebook* (New York: Families and Work Institute, 1988).

2. James T. Bond, Ellen Galinsky, and Jennifer E. Swanberg, "Executive Summary," *The 1997 National Study of the Changing Workforce* (New York: Families and Work Institute: 1998) and SHRM Survey Program, *2002 Benefits Survey* (Alexandria, VA: SHRM, 2002).

3. James. T. Bond, Ellen Galinsky, and Jennifer E. Swanberg, "Executive Summary," *The 1997 National Study of the Changing Workforce* (New York: Families and Work Institute: 1998).

4. Ibid., Executive Summary, p. 1.

5. Ibid., p. 12.

6. *The 1998 Business Work-Life Study.*

7. Ibid.

Chapter 16

1. Ellen Galinsky and James T. Bond, "Executive Summary," *The 1998 Business Work-Life Study: A Sourcebook* (New York: Families and Work Institute, 1988).

2. William M. Mercer Inc. and Bright Horizons Family Solutions, *Survey Report: Work/Life Initiatives 2000* (2001).

Chapter 17

1. Joan Williams, *Unbending Gender: Why Family and Work Conflict and What to Do About It* (New York: Oxford University Press, 2000).

2. In 2000, median weekly earnings for female full-time wage and salary workers aged 45 to 54 years was 72.7% of comparable men. In contrast, among those 25 to 34 years old, women's earnings were 81.9% of comparable men's. Among workers 20 to 24 years old, women's earnings were 91.9% of men's. Bureau of Census for the Bureau of Labor Statistics, *Highlight of Women's Earnings in 2000* [Report 952] (Washington, DC: U.S. Department of Labor, 2001), Tables 1 and 8.

DATE DUE